Growing Up in Eighty Four, Pennsylvania
A Slice of Americana

KEITH NEILL

Growing Up in Eighty Four, Pennsylvania
A Slice of Americana
Keith Neill
Copyright © 2016 Keith Neill
All rights reserved.

Unless otherwise noted, all images in this volume are in the public domain.
Sketches and drawings created by Louise Vrable.
The drawing on page 146 is by Elizabeth Jones
Cover design: kayleenburke.com

Growing Up in Eighty Four on the web at: facebook.com/84book

ISBN: 10 1533109125
ISBN-13: 978-1533109125

DEDICATION

These memories of my life in Eighty Four, Pennsylvania are dedicated to my mother who tried to teach me right from wrong. Did she succeed? And to my father who was a true country gentleman.

For Olivia, Carrie and Jay

CONTENTS

1. Seven Rooms and a Path 1
2. Our House 5
3. Laundry 9
4. Number Please 13
5. Brownlee Elementary School 17
6. Sunday Meals 21
7. Family Shopping 23
8. My Dad's Rides 27
9. A Bunch of Hayseeds 31
10. The Escalator 33
11. Tooth Fairy 37
12. My First Wheels 39
13. Surgery At Seven 41
14. The Milkman 45
15. Housecleaning, A Rite of Spring 47
16. The Monster In The Cellar 51
17. Mom, I'm Home 53
18. Cones, Klondikes and the Ice Cream Man 57
19. Home Made Ice Cream 59
20. Life in Black and White 63
21. Maid in the Shade 67
22. The Forbidden Room 71
23. Quilting: an Art 73
24. A Memorable Christmas 75
25. Washington County Fair, 1954 77
26. Washington County Fair, 1954, Part II 81

27. Eighty Four's Coolest Kids 83

28. The Color Barrier 85

29. My Dad, The Farmer 89

30. Making Deposits 93

31. An Unhappy Day on the Farm 95

32. The Mingo Spring House 97

33. Wish Book World 101

34. The Knickerbocker Club 103

35. Miss Trinity 107

36. Heigh, Ho Silver 109

37. Solomon 111

38. The Train, The Rain and My New Hat 113

39. Strawberry Fields Forever 117

40. City Chicken 119

41. On Top of the World 121

42. Park There 125

43. My First Business 129

44. I Got to Drive to School 133

45. Help, The Sky is Falling 137

46. Scary, Scary Night 139

47. Hind Sight 143

ACKNOWLEDGMENTS

I would like to recognize several people who made this book possible. The members of the Monroeville Lifestory Writers, who read and critiqued every chapter. They are a non-threatening group of writers who have offered their knowledge of grammar, sentence structure and general comments to improve the final manuscript. Sharon Lippincott led this group. The New Stanton Writing Workshop members also offered suggestions that led to the improvement of the final edition. I learned things I didn't know about commas, clauses, and complex sentences. These groups have inspired me with their writings and suggestions

Heather Neill Revanna, my daughter who questioned some archaic words, told me about passages that she didn't understand and who offered suggestions. I listened to some and appreciated her zeal for good writing.

To Nancy Clark who has eyes for grammar and structure. She's the old school who learned about structure and grammar in a different era, just like me, except she listened. Thanks, Nancy for your critical eye.

My in house critic, Louise Vrable has been invaluable as a reader who always asks, "What do you mean here?" or "Where is this going?" Thanks, Louise. Your comments have been invaluable. Louise also created most of the sketches in this book.

PREFACE

"Where's Eighty Four?" is a common question when a person from that community is asked where it is located.

The smart answer is, "It's between 83 and 85."

Old timers always got a great laugh out of that answer.

Our family farm is located in central Washington County Pennsylvania. The address was Rural Route 1, Eighty Four, Pennsylvania, but the nearest small village is called Linden.

One day my Dad was listening to the World News with Lowell Thomas, on the radio.

"Dad, why are they always talking about Linden?"

"They're not talking about Linden. It's London," he told me.

At the time, I didn't hear the difference between the two names.

After two years at the one-room Brownlee Elementary, I went to third grade at Linden Elementary School. By that time I had gotten it straight.

I thought our farm was the center of the universe.

My brother Curt and I investigated every inch of the land. We played along the Linden Creek, swam in it and collected minnows there. Sometimes the creek became a place to get a drink. Didn't we know cows used that stream as well? We collected walnuts that stained our hands with the tannin in the hulls. Farm animals became pets. We trained them, loved them and treated them like family. That was a big mistake. One day when we came home from school, one of our farm pets was gone.

Curt and I spent hours entertaining ourselves by making up games and arguing over the rules. A favorite escape was the soft dirt under the front porch where we created large excavations and villages. We never had a lot of toys but we could make do with things we found in the barn or the kitchen. A short piece of two-by-four became a bulldozer. We were never bored.

The dairy farm supported our family's lifestyle.

Weekends were a magnet for visitors—family, friends and neighbors. Many of these people you will meet in the following pages.

These stories will take you from Eighty Four to places around the world. Each chapter is a glance at life in rural western Pennsylvania to the ends of the earth. It all began in Eighty Four, Pennsylvania, a slice of Americana.

1. SEVEN ROOMS AND A PATH

Seven rooms and a path was what we called our farm house. The house had three bedrooms, a country kitchen, a huge dining room and living room, plus a parlor—that was then used as my grandmother's bedroom, but the path was the most used. It went from the back porch, under the grape arbor, around the shrubs and ended at the two-seater. I hated going there in the winter or the dark. My grandmother had a chamber pot that she kept under her bed. It had to be emptied every morning into the outhouse, but it kept her from having to go outside in the middle of the night. This all changed in 1949. We got a bathroom in the house. Yay, it's a new day.

Prior to this, the only running water we had in the house was from the pitcher pump in the kitchen. Water was collected off the roof and it ran through a charcoal filter and into the cistern which was located under the porch. The pitcher pump in the kitchen drew water from that cistern. We did not drink this water. It was pure enough for washing dishes and household cleaning but never for drinking.

Drinking water came from a hand dug well that was located on the back porch. The large hand pump was situated atop the concrete that covered the well. Each day, a new, clean stainless steel bucket of water was pumped and brought to the kitchen to be used for drinking and cooking. In it was a long handled dipper, much like a ladle. It was used to dip water; everyone used this water to clean food to be cooked and to fill pots and pans. A community glass was stashed on the outside kitchen window sill opposite the outside pump. It could be used for a quick drink if you were outside. This water was always at a perfect temperature to drink—no ice needed. It was luscious. We didn't worry about sharing the same glass.

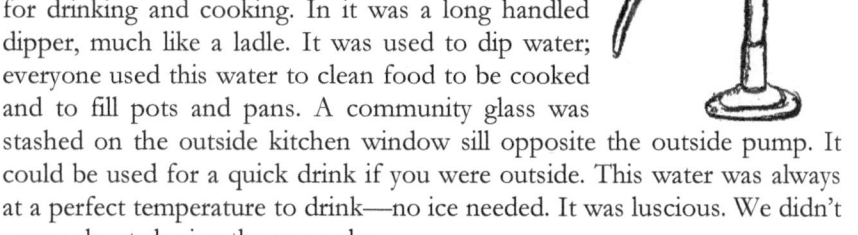

This all changed when my dad had some guys drill a well right outside the dining room window. It supplied enough water for cooking, washing clothes and whatever we wanted to do with water. Now that there was running water we could have a bathroom. I had never taken a bath in a bath tub. To get cleaned up, we heated water on the stove and then put it in a basin. This was for the daily wash up and the clean up before bed. The Saturday night bath happened at the kitchen sink, when I was very young. I was getting too big to do this. I didn't wish to use the wash tub in the hallway, like my mom, dad and grandmother did.

Since there was no room for a bathroom in the house, my dad had to get creative along with his friend Bernard Weaver--they added the bathroom on the roof of the back porch. It was accessible from the landing of the upper stairway. It was small, but it was a bathroom. We now had seven rooms and a bath.

In addition to the upstairs bathroom, we had a shower in the basement and an extra commode, but not an entire bathroom. The shower was located near the washing machine and was great for our hired hands, as well as for us, to wash off.

We even had an outdoor spigot with which we could wash the car and water flowers. We thought we had really made it.

The most noticeable change came in the kitchen. The pitcher pump had to go. The base on which it sat was wooden and needed to be redone. It was removed, totally. Now we had a modern white metal cabinet base that was covered with a stainless steel top, which included an inset stainless sink.

A septic tank over the hill from the house replaced the outhouse. Eureka.

So, now we had water on three floors. But we also had a pipe that ran to the barn. My dad told me that with the pipes running to the barn and the electricity running overhead that we looked like Pittsburgh. The line to the barn allowed water for all the jobs there. Milking equipment and buckets had to be scoured after each milking, twice a day. This had been done in the house before the water ran to the barn. We also had to wash the cows' udders prior to milking. The milk cooler was filled with water to the level just below the top of the five gallon milk cans. A truck came every day to pick it up and take it to a dairy for processing.

Before there was water in the barn, the cows had to be let out of the barn to drink from the creek. It was easier in the summer, but during very cold weather the ice had to be broken so the cows could get enough to drink. They always knew how to find the water. Now a cast iron watering bowl was located between every two stanchions.[1] Each cow could push a lever like paddle with her nose to open the water valve and drink as much

---

[1] The original watering bowls in the barn were purchased, used, from the Bell farm that is now the site of Pittsburgh International Airport. My dad bought them at a public sale when the farm was purchased to build the airport.

water as she needed. When in the house, we could always tell when the cattle had finished eating. Then they needed to drink and we could hear the pump in the basement. It might run for half an hour.

Now we had seven rooms and a bath.

2. OUR HOUSE

Life is nothing without friendship. Cicero

The big old farm house sat up the lane off of the windy country road. It was far from modern and would never qualify for a spread in *House Beautiful,* but it was a magnet for family, neighbors and friends. Our house was the center of the universe, or at least I thought so when I was a kid.

Sunday afternoons were lazy and seemed to be the time that everybody came to visit. Part of this was because my Grandmother Neill lived with us. And did she have the connections! There were cousins, old neighbors, former classmates, former students, and maybe an aunt or uncle of mine. At times there would be three conversation centers—the living room, the dining room and in good weather, the back porch. Somehow the men always ended up on the back porch or under the large maple tree that guarded the end of the clothes line. I thought this happened to all families, but later on I figured it out that we were different; none of the neighbors had this much company. People who came to our house were called company.

There were older ladies with white hair and purple hair and cheeks as red as beets; they all came with their hair in a bun or braids that were wound and pinned close to their head. Rimless octagon glasses were the choice of the retired teacher. None of the women wore slacks; some wore floral-printed dresses that would make great drapes for the Holiday Inn. Others wore "house dresses," and their shoes were black laced oxfords with a slight heel. Even in the hottest weather none of these visitors appeared in shorts.

The men wore clean work clothes — blue chambray shirts were most often the Sunday afternoon dress of the old guys. Either bright green or red suspenders kept their pants in suspense, all this topped off with straw hats, often with a green plastic inset on the front of the brim. Beside the visitors on Sundays we always had people coming to get milk. It was self-serve. They just got the number of gallons that they needed and left the money in the coffee can on the shelf in the corner. They could even make change if they needed to. Some of these customers eventually became part of the neighborly exchange.

Saturdays were my mother's baking day and she always planned extra goodies for the Sunday visitors. Beginning early in the morning there would be a fusion of aromas coming from the kitchen

When we came in from doing our morning barn chores there would be homemade bread, thick fruit pies with juice dripping from the edge, lemon or banana cream pies with mile high meringue, all lined up on the counter like they were going to be judged at the county fair. Sometimes she baked cinnamon rolls oozing with sticky goo and topped with smooth white glaze and sprinkled with chopped nuts. No wonder so many people liked to stop at our house.

I can remember when my friend came into the kitchen and saw the bread rising in an old round aluminum roaster sitting atop the Hoosier cabinet. It had raised the lid in the process and he called to my mother, "Mrs. Neill, your bread is overflowing." The bread would be formed into large loaves baked in a pie pan or a traditional loaf pan. Ketchup that my mother made was so good on this warm bread. The bread was famous and delicious, although I asked my mother if she would buy white "doughy" bread for my school lunch sandwiches so the kids wouldn't tease me. I was the only kid in school who brought home-baked bread in his lunch. None of the visitors at our house ever seemed to care that the bread was homemade, especially when topped with freshly churned butter and newly cooked berry jam.

The ladies in the flowered dresses taught me how to play lots of exciting games. I found out how to play Monopoly, Touring, Checkers, and lots of card games. The battles of these games got heavy at times and I learned about winning and losing. It was valuable training for getting along in the working world. The mustached old guys tried to teach me how to carve a bird from a piece of sweet perfumed pine, but a bloody finger made that a short-lived hobby. The fellow with the Barlow told me I better learn to do some other pastime, like reading a book. The flying pen knife of Mumblety Peg was easier, if the players wore shoes. The pen knife that stuck in the ground closest to the foot was the winner. Ouch.

On special holidays such as Easter, Thanksgiving and Christmas we would set up long tables that spanned from the dining room through the living room. The tables were covered with my mother's best linen table cloth and out came the good china and silverware. Every mismatched chair in the house was placed around the table to accommodate all the hungry aunts, uncles and cousins plus great aunts and uncles, and a special table was set up for the kids. As a kid, I couldn't wait to get to the adult table and then when I got there thought, "What's so great about this?" In later years I volunteered to sit at the kids table. Adults had too many talks about politics and illnesses.

After the feast was over the men sat around the table while the women began to clean up. The silverware always had to be counted when put back into the red felt lined wooden chest. I always wondered if Gram thought that some of the relatives would try to take some.

We didn't know what a family room was, but our dining room table became the center of family life. It was a place to do homework, play games and entertain. Since it connected to the living room, we could easily talk with mom, dad and gram. I can still see Nipper, the RCA Victor radio dog, on the front of the radio dial as we listened to "The Lone Ranger" and "Hopalong Cassidy" in the dining room just before supper. When I finally saw these cowboys on TV, I told my mother, "That's not what they look like."

Growing up in this friendly house allowed me to intimately understand the great give and take of idle conversation; we knew about everybody's comings and goings, their problems and their triumphs. I learned how to listen to everyone and to ask my own questions. I didn't always get all the nuances of the conversation because there were subjects that were frequently off limits to kids my age. When I asked a question that was over the edge, the adults would tell me that they didn't want to talk about it anymore. I didn't push it.

All this took place in a house that didn't have a bathroom until I was six. But that didn't keep any of the people from coming to see us. Before my grandmother moved to this house in 1929, she had been invited there to a community square dance. The living room and dining room, which are separated by a massive arch, are each large enough to accommodate a square. She said when she came there to dances she never thought she would live there. I can visualize the fiddle, guitar and upright base playing music for the dance. The bedrooms above these rooms were equally as large. I never realized how large the house was until I lived in an apartment in college.

Maybe the walls could still hear the strains of "Turkey in the Straw" and beckoned the multitudes to stop by and share the bread and trade one more story.

3. LAUNDRY

When I was very young, we didn't have a place to do laundry in the house. We had a washhouse. It was a white, gray trimmed clapboard building with a dinner bell on the peak. This building was located a few steps off the edge of the back porch. It is still there. We still have the washboard, which is a ripple-surfaced board about 18 inches wide on which my Gram rubbed wet clothes with soapy water to get them clean. Mom did too.

Pump the water till the bucket's full. Carry the bucket up the step. Pour it into the oval copper boiler—repeat till the boiler is full. Light the gas under the boiler. Set up the rinse area, a galvanized square was the tub. Bring the oval wicker basket of clothes from the house. Sort the clothes into four piles—whites, light colors, dark colors and dirty work clothes. The 18-foot-deep hand dug well provided water for cooking, drinking and washing clothes.

Every Monday my mother or grandmother could be seen hauling the baskets of dirty clothes out of the house and up the three steps into the washhouse. Then I can remember one of them carrying galvanized, square tubs of water from the outside pump to the 'laundry,' where it was heated, to boiling. These mavens of the washhouse believed that water had to be boiling to get clothes clean. Sometimes they even boiled the clothes in the copper boiler. I wasn't allowed near the boiler. There were horror stories of kids who been scalded on wash day. When I was old enough, I had to pump and carry the water to the washhouse, but I was never allowed near the hot water.

The Maytag washer lived in the washhouse. My Aunt Hazel worked as a bookkeeper at the Maytag store in Washington, Pennsylvania, so she was able to get a good deal on this machine. It replaced the washboard that had been used to wash clothes until that point. These were the days when doing the laundry was truly a job, an all day job.

Once the water came to a boil, it was transferred to the Maytag, with buckets. The white clothes were placed in the washer once it was filled with water. A combination of bought soap powder and homemade lye soap was added. These washer women didn't think that bought soap had the power of homemade lye soap. Maybe that's why I hesitated to have a new shirt placed in the wash. Lye soap had the power to fade brightly colored clothes and make them look old after one washing.

The agitator in the middle of the washer had to be activated by a lever that resembled the floor gear shift from our old pickup truck. The washer operator shifted this into the mode where it agitated the clothes for ten to fifteen minutes. When the lady of the laundry decided that the clothes had agitated long enough to remove the dirt, a short stick, the remains of an old broom stick, was used to collect the clothes from the hot water in the machine. The gear shift was moved to stop agitation while the clothes were being removed.

The clothes were then squeezed through the wringer, which is made of two rubber rollers, a little larger than two rolling pins. The rollers have a gear and they can operate in two directions. Clean clothes from the washer pass through the wringer and fall into the tub of cold water for rinsing. After the rinse, the ringer can swivel and then the rinsed clothes pass through the wringer again and then fall into the clothes basket, ready for the clothes line or the dryer.

Once the whites were done, the water that had been used to wash the white clothes remained in the washer and the next lightest clothes were washed in the same water. This procedure continued until the darkest and dirtiest clothes were washed last, in the same water. Often times it was the men's farm work clothes and throw rugs that came last. When the final load was washed and the washer was drained often times the dirt that had been washed from rugs could be found in the bottom of the washing machine.

Drying was easy on summer days when it didn't rain. There were heavy gauge wire lines that ran from the edge of the house to a pole at the end of the yard. Before hanging the clean clothes, the lines had to be cleaned with a wet rag. If it appeared that rain was coming, we didn't wash clothes or they had to be hung inside. The clean clothes were hung over the line and clothes pins secured them to the line so that if it was windy they didn't fall off the line.

In the winter clothes had to be hung inside all the time. For the inside drying, there were two folding wooden racks (we still have them). They were placed in the hall way and the clothes were draped over the wooden rods. No clothes pins were needed. They dried quickly in the house because of the dry heat coming from the coal furnace in the basement. The drying process also added moisture to the dry house air.

In 1949 this all changed, when the deep water well was drilled beside the house. Dad had a portion of the basement dug out that had previously been crawl space under the family dining room. Once the dirt was removed, the floor was cemented. An electric water pump brought the underground water to the holding tank and a gas hot water heater was added. The entire washing procedure changed. The Maytag moved from the wash house to live in the new basement. Water didn't need to be heated in the boiler. The washing procedure remained much the same as it was before, except now a hose could be used to fill the washer and the rinse tub. The dirty water from the washer and the rinse water emptied down the drain. It was almost like it was automatic.

Ironing started on Tuesday, after the clothes were sprinkled.

4. NUMBER PLEASE

The telephone was large and black and it sat atop a small decorative table along the center wall of our living room. I was six the first time I was allowed to pick it up and call somebody. "Number please." Now what do I do? "I don't have a number. I just want to talk to Jim." The operator said, "One moment please." I had heard my grandmother make calls like this many times. She would just ask for my aunts by name and the operator would connect her. Everybody was assigned a phone number. The bank was 1000. My aunt was 5032R11 and ours was 5072J1. When a caller told the operator the number, she made the connection. But she was happy to do it by name if she knew the person.

This was 1949 when all we had were party lines. There were anywhere from four to eight phones, all using the same line. On our party phone line were the: elementary school, the natural gas pumping station, the local constable and a couple of families. We knew everyone on our party line with the exception of one family. We were surprised that Gram hadn't found out who they were. Come on, Gram. Sometimes when you picked up the phone to call you would hear someone talking. That was the busy signal. The talker might say, "I will be off the line soon." If it was an emergency, you could explain that and the person would get off right away to free up the line.

In order to know if the call was for us, we had to listen to the number of rings. Our ring was one long, the school was a long and a short and the gas company was a long and two shorts. That's how you knew when to answer. If my Mother or Grandmother were feeling nosy, they would pick up the receiver when the phone rang for another party. By covering the microphone of the receiver with their hand they could listen to the conversation.

One evening my Mom was on the listening end of a conversation that lasted for nearly an hour. Boy oh boy, was it tough for my brother and me to keep quiet. The constable's son had disappeared from his family's home for nearly a year. There had been a family disagreement between him and his father. The son took off. My family knew this. On this night the "lost son" called to talk with his mother. My mother listened to the entire conversation. The son would be coming home from North Carolina for Christmas. But, you know, my mother couldn't talk to anybody about what she had heard. It was almost like peeking at Christmas gifts. Who are you going to tell?

The party line was really the first answering machine. When Mrs. Caton, the wife of the natural gas pump station operator, would be going away for the day, she would ask my mother to answer her phone when it rang. My mother might do the same. Imagine that.

There was no dial tone. The person asking for the number you wanted to call was the operator. She was also known as "central." There was no dialing numbers and it was near impossible to make long distance calls from where we lived in the country. Maybe it was just my family's way of conserving.

My Grandmother said that we had a telephone line at our house longer than anyone else in the area. My Dad's family had moved to the farm in 1929 and had always had a party line. Because we lived in the country, a private line was not available. There was no such thing as a busy signal. If you called somebody and their line was in use, the operator would say, "That line is busy." Today's phones have so many features that the old timers would need a class on how to use them. Even in my house today, if the phone is in use, the message on the screen on the other phone reads, "Line in Use."

Mrs. Caton belonged to several social clubs and was a participant in several groups at the local church. My Gram was in a similar situation. She belonged to at least two clubs and three organizations in the church. In addition to this, Gram wrote the local news that appeared in two newspapers. Mrs. Caton was always a good feed for the local news column. But when we wanted to call her, we had to tell the operator her number and then hang up. When we could hear that the phone was no longer ringing we knew that Mrs. Caton had answered her phone. Then we could pick up our receiver and talk with her.

This all ended in 1955. We all got a dial telephone. Our new phone number was Sherwood 5-3767. When calling someone on our exchange, we dialed the S and the H which we know are 7 and 4. The phone company had designed this arrangement because they said callers would never be able to remember that many numbers. Do you remember the name of your telephone exchange before it went to all number calling (if you're over 60)? How many sets of numbers and passwords do we have to remember now?

~~~~~~~~~~~~

~~~~~~~~~~~~

    I came across another story of how much the world of phones has changed. I learned in the obituaries of the *Tribune-Review* about the death of Father Flavian Yelinko, who was the oldest monk at St. Vincent College in Latrobe, PA. Apparently, when he arrived on campus in 1920 the school had one telephone. It was manned by Brother Jake in the monastery. When he was mowing the lawn, there was no one to answer the phone.

    Father Flavian died on February 18, 2010. He was 103.

    How many phones and cell phones might be on that campus today?

5. BROWNLEE ELEMENTARY SCHOOL

It was the best of times, but we didn't know it yet. We were so nervous and anxious about starting first grade. But as with most new experiences, we were pushing our fingers through our pants pockets as we waited for the bus. Tommy, my closest neighbor, lived in the house up the road from ours and we played together since he moved there earlier in the year. It was good to know someone who would be in the same room. We waited and waited for the bus, but it didn't come. Then along came Mr. White, our neighbor; he stopped and asked, "You boys waiting on the bus?"

"Yeah! Where is it? I think it's late."

"I saw it go by about ten minutes ago. I know I saw it go. Do you want me to take you to school?"

"Well, I guess so." Tommy said.

"Get in. I'll take you. I'm just doing some remodeling at your house, so your mom and dad won't be too upset if I'm a little late."

We got to school shortly after the bus had arrived and it was really not a problem, but we were twice as nervous about the first day of school.

This was the first year Mrs. Johnson would not be teaching eight grades. The community was growing and the one room school would now house only first and second grades. The other kids were now going to the old high school which would be for grades third through eighth.

Brownlee Elementary resembled most one room schools in the area. It was a white clapboard rectangle with a bell tower on the front. Three cement steps led to the vestibule and furnace room which connected to a pleasant classroom with stationary wooden and metal desks, bolted to the floor. The back of the first seat served as a writing and storage area for the next person as they lined up like soldiers at attention in eight rows. Seats folded up for cleaning, which Mrs. Johnson did at the end of the day. Tall windows with large blinds and air deflectors were on two sides of the building. The thought was to let plenty of light into the room on cloudy days. The other side was a solid wall with slate chalk boards and a bulletin board at the top where the printed and cursive alphabets were displayed.

The building was situated on a lot about the size of a baseball field.

Behind the school was a girls' outhouse and to the far right of the school was another for the boys. Children could wash their hands in the vestibule area right next to the water fountain. Everyone had to line up after lunch play time and after recess, which was a time to let off steam.

The school grounds gently sloped to a small stream. We were permitted to play along the stream. On more than one occasion we collected minnows and brought them to the classroom. I don't believe they were able to read "Dick and Jane." They did adorn the top of the bookshelf. They weren't there the next day.

There was no lunch room. A cloak room joined one side of other classroom. Hooks provided a cozy place for coats, leggings[2] and boots. The lower shelf was the storage area for the home packed lunch that everyone carried to school each day. Each student picked up their lunch from the cloak room and took it to their desk to eat. Later in the year we were able to buy cups of soup à la Heinz. It was ten cents per cup until the electric soup cooker was paid for and then it was five cents per cup. Mrs. Johnson opened the cans and put the soup on to heat. The second grade girls washed the spoons each day. I was seldom allowed to buy.

Mrs. Johnson wore many hats. She was the janitor, the nurse, the cook, the counselor and the secretary, but most of the time she was the best teacher. She did have a little help. The biggest boys were called into action to carry in the coal from the nearby shed and to carry out the ashes from the furnace. The boys were not permitted to add coal to the furnace or to remove the ashes from the under portion.

The day started with Mrs. Johnson reading a passage from the Bible, after which we students recited the Lord's Prayer and the Pledge to the flag. We also sang the first verse of "My Country 'Tis of Thee." Mrs. Johnson had a solo until we learned the words.

Because we were in first grade, we didn't get any books right away. Mrs. Johnson had a "big book" that sat on an easel in the front of the classroom. It had stories about "Dick and Jane." We also received white pages with purple printing that she had produced using a hectograph. The hectograph was a machine that used a glycerin-coated layer of gelatin to make copies of typed or written material. After removing the master copy, she had to press each page onto the gel surface, smooth it with her hand and then peel each off, one at a time. We didn't get too many of these copies. She also gave us pre-printed pages that accompanied the big book.

We often memorized short passages from a reading workbook. One

---

[2] Leggings in the late 1940s were different from today's leggings. Girls were not allowed to wear pants to school, and so they had leggings which matched their coats; these were worn as outerwear.

such passage was:
> One two, buckle my shoe,
> Three, four, shut the door,
> Five, six, pickup sticks,
> Seven, eight, lay them straight,
> Nine, ten, a big fat hen.

We got to use the hand outs and number practice sheet while Mrs. Johnson taught the second grade students. It was interesting to hear the lesson of the second grade's class because they could already read. I really learned to read just by listening to their lesson. First and second graders had art, music and physical education together. Christmas and spring programs were also a joint venture.

But the first day became very interesting during the afternoon recess. As we explored the new playground, someone said, "There's an Indian."

"No, there are no Indians around here."

"Yes there are. My brother told me there's a lot of them around."

"Let's get out of here. He's after us."

Just then the large bell atop the building began ringing. It was time to go back to the classroom to finish the first day's activities.

There was a lot of buzz when we returned to the classroom and Mrs. Johnson had to remind us of the classroom rules that she had explained that morning.

"Only one person can talk at a time, please, and raise your hand if you want to say something," she reminded us. "What happened that everyone is so excited?"

"We saw an Indian in the woods behind the school."

"Tell me what he looked like," she probed.

"He had a band around his head with a feather," Joe said.

"And he had war paint on his face," Sandy added.

"Did he say anything?" Mrs. Johnson wanted to know.

"No, he didn't, "Tommy said. "I don't think he speaks English, my mom says they speak Indian."

At that point, one of the second graders raised her hand.

"Yes, Louise."

"I think that's my brother. He loves to dress up and play Indian." What color was his hair?"

"It was blond," Sandy said.

"Indians don't usually have blond hair," Mrs. Johnson added.

"I know that's my brother," Louise said. "He'll be in first grade next year."

"Wow!" Tommy said. "That sounds like fun."

"Maybe we can play Indian some day, too. Let's do it tomorrow," Joe added.

Mrs. Johnson went on to explain that Louise's home was just through the woods and facing the road around the corner.

"Now we must finish the art lesson before dismissal time."

It had been an exciting day and the beginning of a fun school year. Every day brought excitement and great educational experiences.

6. SUNDAY MEALS

I don't know how my mother did it. No frozen entrees. No instant mashed potatoes. No frozen desserts and no pizza delivery. Really, we didn't even know what pizza was. Every meal at our house was homemade, even our bread. But Sunday meals were special in their own right, though not quite like Thanksgiving and Christmas. I like to think of them as mini holiday meals.

My mother must have gotten up before the chickens, labored through the kitchen preparing as much food as she could before we left for church, every Sunday. She traipsed to the basement to retrieve potatoes that we had grown and stored in the fruit cellar. We knew what real mashed potatoes were. Sometimes they even had lumps.

One of the spring chickens that had lived and walked the farm was put into to the pot to pre-boil. When we got home from church the chicken was dredged in flour and two herbs and spices—salt and pepper and then put into a large iron skillet, sizzling with butter. Eat your heart out, Colonel Sanders. Other favorites were Swiss steak, or pork roast, and sometimes pork chops. But the frying was done in the large iron skillet. Yum.

Swiss steak and the pork main dishes were also prepared ahead of time, almost like the chicken. What time did she get up?

When we got home from church, Mom donned a granny print apron that covered her church clothes, as she continued the Sunday dinner preparation.

She had to wait to make the gravy till we got home. Luscious yellow gravy came with the chicken. It was made from the broth left from cooking the chicken. She claimed it had its bright yellow color, because the chickens searched the great outdoors to fortify their bodies with natural vitamins and minerals they found among the bugs and plant life. I didn't know to call them free range chickens.

The gravy spilled over the mounds of mashed potatoes when we served ourselves from the large pottery serving dishes. On alternating Sundays the brown gravy from the steak tantalized our taste buds. We didn't need an appetizer. Aromas of any of these foods wafting through the kitchen and dining room were all that we needed to activate our appetites and say "come to dinner."

In addition to the potatoes we had other home grown vegetables. In summer, bright yellow corn was picked from the field just prior to cooking. After harvest season we had either canned or frozen corn that had only been out of the corn field about 30 minutes before it hit the boiling pot of water.

My dad used to say: put the water on to boil, hike off to the cornfield, pick the corn, husk it and head back to the house. He said if we fell down while carrying the corn to the kitchen, it would be too old to eat.

Green beans were the other common vegetable. We had planted them, tilled them all summer, and picked them and cleaned them on Saturday night. They were a favorite, cooked in the southern style, with either ham or bacon. These beans, like the corn were also preserved for the winter use.

When we canned beans, we did them by the bushel. After cleaning and washing them, we packed them in Mason jars. We added water and salt, closed them and placed them in the copper boiler that held 18 quart jars. You just add enough water to surround the jars, place the boiler lid and boil on the basement hot plate for three hours. *We loved them in the winter.*

Other regular seasonal vegetables that came from the backyard garden were: broccoli, cauliflower, tomatoes, beets and zucchini.

The additional popular dish, usually served only on Sundays was red Jell-O™ with fruit cocktail. My Dad called it "thickened wind." It's hard to believe that my mother spent money to buy Jell-O and fruit cocktail.

And then there was dessert. Everyone in the family seemed to have a sweet tooth. Baking pies was Mumsie's specialty. She had learned well from my Grandmother Myers.

Both Gram and my Mother were experts at taking the seasonal fruits and converting them into luscious pastry desserts. Dad's favorite was apple pie. Of course, he picked the apples. We had no less than fifty trees to choose from. During other seasons, she made pies from the fruit that was in season—berries, peaches, cherries and pumpkin. My favorite was the one where my mother made vanilla pudding. It was put in an already-baked crust and topped with meringue and coconut, all toasted under the broiler—coconut cream pie.

On Sunday evening, my Mom took it easy. We nearly always had grilled cheese sandwiches and cocoa. The sandwiches were prepared in the Griswold™ griddle, swimming with butter and cheese oozing out from between the slices of bread. This meal had to be a snap for my mother after what she had done each Sunday morning. Of course there was leftover Jell-O and dessert.

7. FAMILY SHOPPING

My mother taught me many of the things that I would never learn in school. One of my most pleasant memories was going shopping in Washington, Pennsylvania on the day that the milk check came. Mom taught me to make a list, go to the shop where the item is sold and buy it. The day before the shopping trip, we sat down at the table and discussed what we needed to buy in town. We could save time, spend less money and not make any impulse buys. We didn't spend a lot of time on touchy-feely shopping. To this day, I still don't like to shop. I go, make my purchase, and go home.

The milk check was our pay day. The main farm product was milk and the dairy sent a check once a month. The first stop in town was the Washington Union Trust where the family banked for years. It eventually became the Pittsburgh National Bank (PNB) and ultimately PNC Bank. As a child I was mesmerized by the intricate workings of the vault while Mom took care of the money stuff. The vault door was larger than a garage door and swung on huge hinges with gears and mechanisms that came together to lock it after each business day. *I wanted to go in the vault, but I was afraid the door would swing shut and I'd be locked in there.* I was much older when I was able to go into that vault with Mom to open the family lock box. Portable ramps came out each business day to keep "lock box lookers" from walking on the cogged wheels that emerged from the floor when the vault door closed.

"Come on, they'll lock you in there," she told me as a kid. I really could have spent more time trying to figure out how the vault device worked.

"Do we have to go?"

"Yes, you know your Dad doesn't like to wait around."

Mom's next stop, with cash in purse, was the Washington Meat Market, the only store in the area that sold Hills Brothers Coffee. All the family coffee drinkers believed that it was the only coffee that could satisfy their caffeine deprived palate.

J.C. Penney was the main store where we bought family clothes.

Depending on the season, we stopped there for new school clothes, winter coats, sale items—not every week—and barn clothes. Who knew that my denim barn coat would eventually become a fashion trend? I loved Penney's because the clerks didn't have cash registers. They put the customer's payment into a small container that resembled a small trolley. It traveled on a track up the wall and into a hole in the ceiling. "Wow! That is so cool. Where does it go?" And just as quickly, the same little tram returned. The clerk opened it and handed change to my mother. Watching the little trolleys from various parts of the store racing from cashier to sales clerk became my favorite indoor sport of this part of the shopping experience.

"Come on. We have places to go," my Mother said as she gripped my hand and headed out.

New shoes came from Brown's Boot Shop—next to Penney's. A nice gentleman measured my foot and brought several pairs from which I could pick one. Mom knew the man who worked there and he catered to our needs. He knew that this was the only place we bought shoes.

But the most time was spent in G.C. Murphy. It was huge compared to the F.W. Woolworth, the five-and-ten that was next to the bank. Murphy's was the choice compared to Woolworth's, because of their larger selections. Mom would buy oil cloth to cover the kitchen work table. Oil cloth is a close woven cotton or linen material that is coated with boiled linseed oil. It was a predecessor of plastic, but it cracked as it aged and often had to be replaced. She bought thread, embroidery floss, and dresser scarves. She used the floss to create beautiful linens that were embroidered into striking dresser linens. In Murphy's basement she surveyed the kitchen items like scouring pads, dish washing cloths, and a new white enamel dish pan.

Murphy's even had a huge eating area consisting of a counter with tall stools and several booths. At the counter we got a sandwich, a drink or on rare occasions, an entire meal. This area was the go-to place for town workers, shoppers, and kids. Prices were reasonable, and they served tasty home style foods as well as snack foods that shoppers could eat on the run. The coconut cream pie had the tallest meringue that we'd ever seen.

Chrome legged kitchen chairs lined both sides of the stairwell to the Murphy's basement store. The chairs were the *after shopping* meeting place for our family and most town shoppers. When Gram came with us, her last stop was at Murphy's candy counter. The uniformed server dropped Gram's selected chocolates or gum drops into the weighing pan of a balance scale and told Gram her cost. We all got to share in the sweets in the white bag. In those days you could ask for ten cents worth and get enough to satisfy your urge for candy. We could find Gram as she munched on her chosen sweet, waiting with other tired shoppers. *Was she the role model for my sweet tooth?*

Gram had spent most of her time at Marshall's Dry Goods Store.

Marshalls had three floors with yard goods, thread, needlepoint canvases, and most sewing supplies that she might need. When I went with her, I liked to watch the stern older lady who cut fabric. She wore half glasses and always had a pencil stuck in her plaited hair. She slid the edge of the material through a machine and a clock-like dial moved around as it measured the exact number of yards of broad cloth, wool, or ticking that Gram had asked for. The older woman made me uneasy—it was the way she looked at me, like I didn't belong there.

"Please pay the cashier on the first floor."

Mom, Gram, Curt and I had covered the entire area in less than an hour. Dad usually drove to the edge of town to buy parts for repairing farm equipment. We all had this shopping completed like an "Olympic event," losing no time and meeting or re-convening if needed.

The big trek was yet to come. We all walked another block to the end of Main Street and turned onto Beau Street. The A & P (The Great Atlantic and Pacific Tea Company) was one block down this street. Here, Mom bought foods to supplement our garden-raised produce and home-canned fruits and vegetables. She got flour, sugar, fish and foods that we didn't produce at home. Curt and I liked hot dogs, which Mom would rarely buy because Dad wouldn't eat them. He had toured a meat packing plant at one time where they were making them. That's why he ate leftovers while we enjoyed the hot dog treat.

At Penney's, we knew several sales people. In Murphy's, we had gotten to know several from many years of shopping in Washington. We were treated like "real people." We asked about their family and they inquired about ours. It was a pleasant shopping experience.

We didn't know what impulse buying was.

"Mom, can I get this notebook?" I begged in Murphy's.

"You don't need it. You have tablets at home."

"Please can't I get it?"

"Quit whining or you can go sit with Gram."

That ended that. Sometimes it worked and I got what I asked for.

Dad drove to the last stop, the Washington Ice House, which was a food locker and meat processing company. After Dad slaughtered a steer, these people cut it and stored it in a small freezer cube that we rented. Folks didn't have a freezer at home; neither did we. We also stored home grown vegetables and fruit in our locker. I loved going into the frozen hallways in the summer. Mom took home foods that fit the next week's menu.

Then we could go home.

This all changed in 1963 when the first shopping area was developed outside of town. It included the K-Mart, Kroger's, a shoe store, a dry cleaner and Mellon Bank. This expansion out of town signaled the beginning of the end of shopping in town. We only knew one person who worked at K-Mart and the check-out people seemed to change every week.

Nobody asked about our family.

8. MY DAD'S RIDES

My earliest memory of riding in the 1941, four door, Chevy sedan, was going to buy groceries with Mom and Dad. I climbed onto the running board and crawled up on to the back seat. Sliding across the brush-like fabric was like sliding across Velcro. With no booster seat, I could hardly see out the side window, but I could help my dad navigate by standing and holding onto the back of the front seat.

After much shopping and walking around town, I frequently fell asleep during the ride home. All I could think about was stretching out on the back seat to take a nap. The upholstery felt like needles pressing against my skin and left an imprint on my cheek and arm when I awakened.

By the time I was seven or eight I was developing car awareness and I was sensitive that the Chevy was beginning to look pretty bad. It was rusting and looked like metal eating termites had gotten to it. In the summer Curt and I would wash it. At this point, it might have been better to leave it dirty; the dirt covered the rust.

In 1952 a new dark blue, four door Chevy Deluxe sedan came to live at our house. It was a six cylinder, with a standard shift on the column. Dad bought the car at Yenko Chevrolet in Canonsburg. In 1952, turn signals were an option. My dad added them, but he didn't get a radio. He knew it would be a distraction—my brother and I later learned to drive on this car. When I drove this car to college 11 years later, I laid my transistor radio on the dash for the one hour round trip.

Dad had a succession of cars after this; a Dodge that he acquired when a neighbor quit driving, and an auto mechanic's Chevy which rusted because it hadn't been undercoated.

Mr. E.J. Keller of Ruffs Dale was the oldest Chevy dealer in the United States. His dealership was at the end of my road. He didn't have to pay General Motor for a showroom car until it sold. Today dealers must pay immediately. When Mr. Keller retired in the mid-1970s, General Motors gave him an olive green Chevy Sedan, but he still had an eye for sales, so he sold it. My dad bought it.

Dad traded that green car for a new Chevy. I had the pleasure of going with Dad to buy his 1984 Chevy Impala. We didn't know at the time, but this would be the last car that he would buy. This time we went to Sun Chevrolet, which is the successor of the Yenko dealership. We knew Howard, one of the salesmen, so we asked for him.

My dad wasn't into having a car sold to him. He knew what he wanted. That's where I had to put my nose into things and have him buy a car that had some style and some modern extras. He settled on a silver gray Impala. I had to encourage him to order the dark red, upgraded interior.

When it came to the radio, Dad said that he didn't need one. Howard encouraged him to get a radio and I agreed. I'd have to drive this car part of the time and I liked to listen to music or keep up with the news and sports. After explaining the various options with tape players, and fancy stereos that were available, Dad settled on an A.M. radio. Hey, at least he got a radio. Because of the small number of gadgets that he wanted on this car, none was in stock, so the car had to be ordered.

Then it came time to talk about money. Howard started the process of listing the new car price and going through the agonizing procedure of asking, "Frank, what will it take to get you to buy this car today?"

Dad told him he came to buy a car. As an aside to me, he wanted to know why Howard was asking that question. I told him it was all part of the sales procedure.

"I don't know why he'd ask me a question like that when I told him I came to buy a car."

"Dad, that's just the way they sell cars today."

"Why do they think I came here?"

"Like I told you, that's just the way they sell cars today."

After Howard and Dad agreed on a price for the car, the fireworks started.

"How much do you plan to give me as a down payment?" Howard asked.

Howard seemed to know that Dad was a little irritated, so he made himself scarce and Dad and I had some frank talk, and not because my Dad's name was Frank.

He looked at me and asked, "Why do I have to give him a down payment. Doesn't he trust me?"

"I guess a lot of people talk to a salesman and let him think they'll buy a car, and then they don't. When you give him money, he'll know you're serious." I told him.

"I've known Howard since he was a kid. His dad was a friend of mine. Isn't my word good enough for him?"

"Maybe he's gotten stuck with a car before."

"How much do I have to give him?"

"Let's ask him."

Dad was used to dealing with farmers whose word was good and a deal was sealed with a handshake.

A down payment of $50 was agreed on and Dad wrote a check. I don't know what the procedures are for this type of transaction, but I think Howard should have covered the $50 himself and adjusted the sale price.

Dad liked the car and I remember going with him to the 100th Anniversary of Eighty Four, Pennsylvania in his new car. It was a proud moment. I sat in the back seat and my Dad and Mom were in front, just like the old days of the 1941 Chevy.

After Dad died, the car became Mom's. Since she didn't drive, my brother Curt or I would take her for groceries or to the doctor in "her" Chevy. It remained Mom's car for six years with Curt or me chauffeuring her. In 1993, the car was sold to my Aunt Hazel who drove it for another ten years.

It was a sad day in 2004 when we saw Aunt Hazel driving up in a used Buick.

Good-bye, Chevy.

9. A BUNCH OF HAYSEEDS

I never thought about what a hayseed was until I was with my Dad at an eye doctor's appointment at the Jenkins Arcade in downtown Pittsburgh. I was six or seven years old. When the receptionist asked him for our address, he responded with the rural Eighty Four address.

"You're just a bunch of hayseeds," she told him.

"I don't know about that," he responded. "

He proceeded to ask her if she had a phone, electricity, natural gas and so on. He didn't tell her that we'd just gotten running water one year earlier. The conversation continued and she felt at that point maybe we weren't hayseeds.

We returned to our seats in the waiting area and I asked, "Dad, what's a hayseed?"

"Hayseed is a word that city folks call people who live in farm country, especially farmers."

"Are we hayseeds?" I continued.

"I don't think so," he went on.

As the school year wound down, I looked forward to summer, but not the dirty work of putting up hay. Hay is made from alfalfa, grasses, clover or other legumes. This is where I learned the real meaning of hayseeds. They are the part of the hay that stuck to me in the hot, sweaty summer. They are the seeds which perpetuate the hay crop.

The entire school calendar was organized around the farm community and the fact that children were needed on the farm to help with the chores. Our farm was no different. My brother, my cousins and I were part of the summer help needed during the haying season.

The summer hay harvest changed drastically during my years of growing up on the farm at Eighty Four. When I was five, the hay was picked up loose. It was cut and allowed to lay on the ground to dry. Hay time then looked like a parade with a tractor pulling a wagon followed by the hay loader, which dropped the windrowed hay on the back of the wagon. Our hired man spread it evenly on the wagon.

The full wagon was hauled to the barn and unloaded with a large hay lifter that resembled the arcade game where you grab a plush animal with a large claw. A rope pulley, drawn by a horse, lifted the claw which was loaded with hay to the loft of the barn. The hay was then released and spread. In the winter the hay was pushed down a chute for the animals to eat. Did I say labor intensive?

In 1950, the hay baler came to our farm. It was hooked behind the tractor, where it picked up the loose hay and shaped it into a rectangular cube, tied it with twine[3] and extruded it onto the ground. Since these bales were scattered over the field, Curt and I rolled them into rows. Dad didn't have small gloves for us so we'd often get splinters in our fingers from twine. This was hard work for little kids. My Dad never heard of child labor laws.

Each 60 to 100 pound bale was loaded onto a wagon and hauled to the barn. The process was easier and the hay bales could easily be loaded and unloaded.

This entire haying process continued on our farm until the 1990s when a newer type of baler came into use. This machine wrapped the loose hay into a compacted roll similar to a jelly roll. These bales can weigh between 600 and 800 pounds. They are so tightly compacted that they don't have to be stored inside. The elements do not penetrate the bale. These bundles of hay must be moved with a device that is attached to the tractor, due to their weight. The hay is placed in an area either in a field or under a pavilion where the cattle can eat at their leisure.

We never had the time to enjoy the public swimming pool, the playgrounds or the evening carnivals that my school friends enjoyed. But we did have Linden Creek where we could escape in the early evening.

Very few hayseeds are left to stick to the sweaty, sun tanned skin of the young kids on today's farm. I guess they have more time to play computer games.

---

[3] Earlier hay balers used wire. Haywire, left over from the hay bales was used to make temporary repairs to many things, hence came the expression, something's gone haywire, as being out of kilter.

10. THE ESCALATOR

Trips to Pittsburgh often became adventures. Where else could I watch a wrecking ball knock down some old sky scraper? I didn't know at the time, but it was part of the Pittsburgh Renaissance! For two years, every Thursday, I went for eye therapy at the Jenkins Arcade. But at times we went to department stores and they had ESCALATORS!

Wow! Gee! Golly! Escalators! I was six when I finally overcame my fear of getting on the clanging, antiquated, wooden, moving stairs that were in some of the downtown stores. Some adult always had to remind me of the danger of getting on the escalator. No store in Canonsburg or Washington had an escalator. Our stores had elevators that were operated by a human being. J.C. Penney and Murphy's had long, wide stairways, but no escalators. These escalators had wide slats that scared me. The wide wooden pieces made clicking and clacking noises that said, *I eat little kids, I eat little kids, I eat little kids,* as the moving stairway crawled into the floor and reappeared on the next level. It looked like it could grab my foot and pull it into the mechanism. OUCH! At first my Dad would hold my hand and remind me not to step on the crack between each step. I thought I was pretty cool when I was able to get onto and off without the help of an adult. I got pretty cocky—I would even jump off as I came down. Sometimes I didn't even hold onto the moving handrail that looked like a great place to play with toy cars. For some reason, I never had a toy to run on the moving hand rail.

Sometimes we would visit my Grandfather's cousins, two old maids, who lived in Dormont. The sisters, Helen and Eva Neill were good at showing us around the city and exposing us to the many experiences that Pittsburgh had to offer. My dad drove me to their house on a Saturday morning. Miss Helen and I took the street car to downtown. Once she found out that I liked the escalator, we went to the top floor of Kaufmann's all the way on the moving stairway. How cool were we? Then we rode back down. Wow! We also went to Horne's and rode the escalator, but not to the top floor. It was a wonderful day. After some shopping and a ride on the street car to Miss Helen's house, we went back to Eighty Four. It had been a great day.

When I got home, I saw a brand new Allis Chalmers combine in the barn. It was huge, about the size of two cars parked side by side and had to be parked in the barn because the machine shed was not large enough to hold it. Threshing, using teams of horses, was going by the wayside. My Dad and his brother, Uncle Judson, had just brought the new combine home. My brother and I thought it would be a great plaything.

Sunday afternoon, the day after I had been to Pittsburgh, Curt and I were at loose ends. I was telling him about the escalators in Pittsburgh when we got the bright idea that the slope of the combine looked like the escalator. We took turns running up and down and jumping off the end of the intake table. On about the fifth time down, I caught my bare foot in the wedge shaped cutting bar.

"Hey Curt, my foot slid in here, I'm caught."

I pulled my foot out. Blood was everywhere. I was too stunned to cry. My brother disappeared, mostly because he's squeamish at the sight of blood.

I hobbled to the house, with blood trickling a path in the dirt and on the grass. I began hollering, "Mom, Mom! Come here! Hurry! I'm bleeding!"

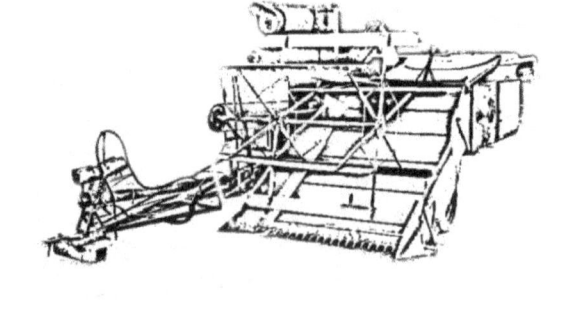

When she saw my foot and all the blood, she called my dad, "Frank, hurry! Come here!" as she ran to get a towel to wrap around it.

When my dad saw the blood soaked cloth, he ran to get the car to take me to the doctor.

"Gram, call Dr. Wilson in Canonsburg!"

We weren't going to an emergency room. We were going to the doctor's office. It was in a three story building sandwiched between a shoe store on the first floor and the pool hall on the third floor. My dad carried me up the wide stairway where Dr. Wilson and his wife met us. As I sat waiting for the doctor to prep my foot, we heard the crack of pool sticks against pool balls and it sounded like thunder rolling above.

"What's that noise?" I asked.

"There's a war on the third floor." Dr. Wilson told me.

Somehow I didn't believe him.

When the doctor unwrapped my blood soaked foot, he could see a big gash across my left arch.

"Do you think I should cut it the rest of the way off?"

"NO WAY!"

"Looks like you're going to need some stitches. I guess we'll sew it back together."

"Will it hurt?"

"I'll numb it so it doesn't."

As Dr. Wilson was stitching the gash in my foot, I realized he only had one leg.

I asked him, "What happened to your leg? Did you lose it in the escalator?" He didn't answer.

I don't remember that the sewing hurt; I do remember that I didn't like the tetanus shot that I got from his wife, the nurse. She jabbed my arm; I hit her arm.

Then he and his wife wrapped my foot in gauze and he told me to stay off of it for a couple of days. Dad carried me back to the car.

Dad told me on the way home that Dr. Wilson had lost the leg because diabetes had taken its toll on his body while he was a soldier in Europe. I don't know why I hadn't noticed the amputated leg previously; after all, Dr. Wilson had administered my smallpox vaccination. In those days it was necessary to show proof of this vaccination before attending public school.

"Dad, what was that noise we heard upstairs in the doctor's office? That wasn't a war was it?"

"No, that was just some guys shooting pool in the pool hall."

I also learned later in life that the pool hall was one of my dad's hangouts in his earlier days.

When we got home, I told dad that I would hop on one leg to the house. I was a hyper kid.

In order to keep me out of further trouble, I was shipped off to Gram Myers' house so she could watch me like a hawk, only she wasn't as attentive as they thought she would be. While Gram did her housework, but I got outside and walked in the mud that surrounded the watering trough.

I never heard Gram Myers so upset. My wound was still healing and I had gotten mud and dirty water soaking into it. Cousin Doris, who is eight years older than I am, took me to the spring house, where the natural cold water flowed. Here she washed the foot and applied a new bandage. It surprises me now that it ever healed. After all, crayfish could be seen swimming in the icy cold water. And was it cold! I can still feel the pain in my foot when I think of that cold water.

I was not permitted to leave the house after this incident. The trip home was the first time I went outside after that.

~~~~~~~~~~~~

~~~~~~~~~~~~

A little side incident occurred about fifty years later. I was wearing rubber overshoes that kept the sole of my shoes from getting wet during snowy weather. While riding the escalator at Westmoreland Mall the giant in the floor snatched one of the overshoes from my foot. It didn't eat little kids, but the mean escalator did run away with my overshoe. There I was walking around the mall with one overshoe. Do you think anyone noticed?

Post Script

When I read this piece at the Monroeville Writers group on June 22, 2011, an interesting thing happened. Helma Weinberg, who was 88 at the time of the reading, and who had been an active duty nurse during World War II shared with the group that she had worked as a nurse at Kaufmann's after her stint with the U.S. Army. Very often she had to treat children who had suffered mishaps while riding the escalators at the store.

11. TOOTH FAIRY

It was a fine Saturday in the summer of 1949 when my dad asked me if I wanted to go along with him and Gram to Pittsburgh. I jumped at the chance to go.

"Sure, I'll go."

We took Gram shopping. She bought a dress at Joseph Horne's. She thought the only place to get a "good" dress was in Pittsburgh—and she was buying a dress to wear to her college class reunion. She graduated from Southwestern Regional State Normal School at California, Pennsylvania. She also bought some sewing supplies—embroidery floss, pillow cases that were to be embroidered, and quilting thread. (I still have the pillow cases that were never embroidered—they are made of cotton and have a price tag of three for $3.85.) We had lunch at the Tea Room before heading to the afternoon of doom. After the shopping, we left Horne's and started across Penn Avenue to the Jenkins Arcade. I went to the Jenkins Arcade every Thursday for eye exercises that were intended to strengthen my eye muscles because I was crossed-eyed.

"Dad, do we have an eye appointment today?" I asked.

"You'll see."

We got in the elevator and got off on the third floor.

"Dad, Dr. Butts isn't on this floor. Why are we here?"

"We're taking you to the dentist."

"Why?"

"I made arrangements to have your tooth pulled."

"I don't want to go."

"Well, you're going."

Had I known this, I would have stayed home. This is when I started getting a lump in my throat and my heart began to pound.

I've had problems with my teeth all my life. I had an extra canine with both my baby teeth and my permanent teeth. My aunt worked at Allegheny General Hospital. She had recommended this children's dentist. It was the usual procedure at the time—*don't tell the child want is happening.*

My mother didn't go with us. I guess she didn't want to witness the pain and suffering.

We arrived at the dentist's office and the assistant took me to the dental chair and prepped me for the procedure. Next the dentist and the anesthetist came with a large mask that was used to administer some type of gas anesthetic that would put me to sleep. I told them that I was not able to breathe and they were trying to suffocate me. I also remember that they reassured me that I was not going to die. These were pretty powerful words to tell a six year old. The next thing I remember about the procedure was awakening with a bad taste in my mouth and one of the assistants wiping my mouth.

Out of the office and off to the car, my father offered to get me some ice cream. It was one of the only times in the world that I refused. Ice cream just didn't seem to be what I needed. Recovery must have been very quick, because I don't remember anything about it. We got home and I asked my dad where the teeth were that had been removed.

"I think the dentist kept them."

"How can I leave them for the tooth fairy?"

"The tooth fairy will know that you had some teeth removed."

"She'd better."

The next morning there was a whole dollar under my pillow.

12. MY FIRST WHEELS

When I was five years old, I wanted a tricycle in the worst way. I had ridden other kids' trikes, but I wanted one of my own. I nagged my mother for days to get me one. I showed her a picture of the one I wanted in the J.C. Penney Christmas Catalog. She had even helped me write a letter to Santa Claus. Her response to all this was, "Where are you going to ride it?"

A couple weeks before Christmas, we went shopping. My mother went to the J.C. Penney basement to get cookie sheets. And there sat my trike in the large Christmas toy display.

"Mom! Mom! This the trike I want. Can I get this?"

"Why don't you ask Santa if he'll bring it? As she pointed to the back wall of the store.

Santa Claus frightened me, but I lassoed my fears and got in the line to talk with him. When it was my turn, I couldn't remember what I wanted to say to him, so I looked at Mom. She realized I had Santa Claus stage fright and said, "Tell him what you want."

"What do I want?" I half whispered to her.

She pointed back to the tricycle. Her cue worked. I proceeded to tell him I wanted a tricycle.

Visiting Santa didn't stop the nagging. I continued to ask my mother, "Do you think Santa will bring it? Do you really think he'll bring me a tricycle?"

"He'll bring it if you've been a good boy."

This means I'll never get a trike.

But on Christmas morning, there it was—the beautiful red and white tricycle, just like the one in at the store.

"Can I ride it?"

"It's too cold. You'll have to wait until warmer weather."

"But I want to try it out."

"O.K., but put on your leggings, your winter coat, hat and boots."

I had my own wheels.

Mom wasn't watching, so I cheated a little. I just put on my coat—the heck with the leggings, boots and gloves. I rode across the dining room, through the kitchen and out the back door onto the back porch. I began to shiver, but I didn't care.

I had a new tricycle and I was going to ride it, no matter the weather. I rode around the back porch a few times. But, as my fingers were turning white and numb, I decided to go back in the house and check out the other loot. I did go out and ride later in the day.

I often rode on warmer days and really took off in the summer. I was the tricycle racer doing laps on our concrete back porch. This was the easiest place to ride. The yard made pedaling difficult and the sloped, red dog drive was as rough as a washboard.

My tricycle got a lot of use for a couple years. My knees were almost biting the handlebars, but I kept on riding. I rode so much that the rubber tire of the back wheel came off. That left a bare rim, but that didn't stop me—no tire, no problem. I could still easily ride on the concrete back porch. Who needs a tire?

Some of the farm cats hung out on the back porch, but they usually scattered when they saw me circling the oval track. The chickens flapped their wings and flew away. We'd had some close calls. I knew something bad had happened when I heard the screeching of the black and white cat as it took off sailing under the grape arbor in the back yard. Its shrieks sounded like the stretching of five screen door springs all at once.

As I came around the next back porch lap, I spotted something that looked like a black feather on the concrete by the cistern. Where did that come from? We don't have any black chickens. Maybe it's a bird feather. It was neither. I didn't realize it at the time, but one of the relaxing felines hadn't tucked her tail when I had rounded the back porch oval track. My tireless tricycle wheel had severed a two inch piece of the cat's black tail. If I hadn't heard the awful noise, I'd never known what happened.

Too bad Wal-Mart didn't exist at that time. If it had happened nowadays we could have taken the cat there. After all, they are the world's largest re**tail**er.

Question: What did the cat say when I ran over its tail?
Answer: It won't be long now.
Groan

13. SURGERY AT SEVEN

No one ever noticed that I was born cross-eyed. I don't know why because when you look at my baby picture, it is quite obvious. My mother told me that was the first time they had become aware of my crossed eyes. I guess no one ever looked into my eyes.

I had seen the ophthalmologist every six months for as long as I could remember. When I think back, this was quite remarkable since I grew up in Eighty Four, Pennsylvania. My grandmother told me the thing that saved me was the fact that George Geeseman, M.D., had been a high school classmate of my father. He became my eye doctor. Now I must tell you, I didn't always like him. He was the guy who held me down and dropped liquid into my eyes. I didn't like the feeling of the drops and I didn't like the dilation that happened with the application of the drops. My father thought the Dr. Geeseman was the greatest. He would heal me because my dad went to school with him.

The medical term for crossed eyes is strabismus. The medical wisdom at the time indicated eye exercises would strengthen my eye muscles enough that I would have straight eyes. Once a week I met with a therapist by the name of Mrs. Butts in the Jenkins Arcade in downtown Pittsburgh, Pennsylvania. For example, Mrs. Butts projected a picture of a pot to one eye and the handle to the other. She moved them in an effort to get my eyes to track the images as they converged on the screen. Sometimes I had to follow a man's hat on to his head. They were cartoon figures.

In addition to the exercises, I had to wear a patch on one eye or the other alternating each day. It was a plastic cup like disc that clipped to my eyeglasses. I wore the patch every day for two years while traveling to see Mrs. Butts every Thursday. I remember often breaking the patch and my parents taping it onto my glasses with whatever tape we had in the house. One time I sported a glowing blue and silver Christmas tape. Thank heavens duct tape hadn't been invented yet. Now it reminds me of my grandchildren insisting that they wear a "Scooby Doo" Band-Aid on a booboo.

I was a "hyper" kid and ended up breaking my glasses every other month. Luckily my uncle's neighbor was an optician and was able to get the studious tortoise shell glasses frames for about two bucks. My glasses resembled Ralphie's of "Christmas Story" fame.

It was a Thursday in February, 1951 when my parents told me that I wouldn't be going to school that day. We were all going to see Dr. Geeseman. I thought nothing of it since it was time to see him, even though I had seen him during the Christmas vacation. The drive seemed longer than usual, since his office was in Mount Lebanon and we had been in the car longer than it took to get there.

I asked my mother what all the tall buildings were and she told my dad to tell me what was going on. He said they are hospitals. Then I asked why we were there. Now I was getting scared. Dad said that Dr. Geeseman would be operating in the morning. My heart sank, I got a lump in my throat and my eyes welled with tears. At this point, I couldn't talk. Neither parent talked either.

They never told me that I was going to the hospital nor did they prepare me for planned surgery. I was seven years old and been a patient of eye doctors from my earliest memory, but I had never been to a hospital.

We had arrived at Eye and Ear Hospital in Pittsburgh. I don't remember much about getting into the hospital. I do remember my mother helping me to put on my pajamas and helping me get into bed. Why do I have to wear pajamas and get into bed in the middle of the day? The attending nurse told me that those were the rules. She was an older stern woman who never smiled. I didn't like her.

I was in a ward that had five beds. There was one in each corner and one straight ahead as you entered the large rectangular room. I don't remember who occupied the other beds. It was all I could do to adjust to this unplanned trip away from my home and my own bed. I had stayed at my grandmother's house, but I had never stayed overnight at a hotel, let alone by myself in a hospital.

Then they presented the biggest shock of the day. My parents told me that they were leaving. My father, a farmer had to complete the farm chores. My bed was next to a high window that looked into the hallway. It was probably designed so that the nurses could "spy" on me. I was never so scared. For the first time in my life, other than school, there would be no family member near me. As mom left, she waved to me through the window. I cried.

I didn't get much to eat and I didn't' want much I was too frightened to eat. I had usually had a thermometer stuck under my tongue, not the way this nurse did it and I had never had blood drawn. There was no preparation for any of the procedures that were happening to me. I was angry at my parents and I wasn't very cooperative with the hospital staff. In spite of this, I did sleep very well.

Friday morning brought more new experiences. I was awakened early and bathed in my bed. This was new to me. Of course, I lived in the country where we didn't even have a bathroom. I was used to the Saturday night bath in a tub in the hallway and a wash up in between, but never in bed. I didn't have any breakfast because of the surgery.

Then a nurse came in and told me that I had to roll on my side because she was going to give me an enema. I told her that I didn't know what that was. She told me that I would make me go to the bathroom. I told her that I didn't have to go and she told me that I had to go now so that I wouldn't go during the operation. Oh well, she won. This was followed by the administration of drop ether to put me to sleep. I was given some type of medication before the ether, probably a sedative, but the mask that was used to administer the ether gave me the feeling of being smothered. I was glad when I went to sleep. That was the last thing I remembered.

I awoke and wondered why it was so dark. I could hear my mother talking and she was holding my hand. "Am I blind?" she told me that both eyes were bandaged. Mom told me that Dr. Geeseman would be coming into the hospital in the evening to remove the bandages. Until then I had to stay in bed and listen to the music that was piped into the room. I also had a younger nurse who was more humane than the one who had been there the day before. This young nurse kept singing "Tennessee Waltz" which Patti Page had recently made popular. My mother and the nurse's aides also read to me. When no one was around to talk to me I would hold on to the sides of the bed for fear that I would fall out.

By now, I was hungry and asked for food. My mother fed me supper. I also had to go to the bathroom and asked her to take me. She asked the nurse to help me get to the bathroom. *RIGHT!* The nurse said that I was NOT permitted to get out of bed. I had to use the bed pan. *RIGHT*, again. Remember, you're trained not to go while you're in bed. Oh boy. Let's just say I was glad my eyes were covered.

Dr. Geeseman was retained somewhere else and didn't come until late in the evening. I heard the doctor and my dad talking. They were discussing the removal of my bandages. Doctor told me it would be very bright when the bandages came off and it was—the brightest light I'd ever seen. It was only a night light. Although it was difficult to see I was never so glad to be able to open my eyes. After my eyes adjusted to the light, the doctor was able to check them out. He told my dad that he had shortened the muscle by five millimeters. I didn't know what he meant, but I knew that I could see very well. I WAS NOT BLIND.

Dr. Geeseman and the nurse bandaged the left eye which was the newly corrected one. I was permitted to go home on Saturday afternoon. The ride home was a joyous one. I told my mom and dad that I never wanted to go to a hospital again. I was given a toy for being such a good patient.

I was allowed to go to Sunday school the next day. The bandage on my eye was a real attention getter. I had lots of questions from the other kids. I told them it was easy to have surgery. *Liar, liar, pants on fire.*

The bandages were removed on the following Wednesday. I still had to wear my glasses until the vision was considered to be 20/20. I remember asking the kids to look at my "new" eyes. I was glad that I didn't have to wear a patch. I was lucky to live where I did and my classmates never teased me.

14. THE MILKMAN

"Sooey cow, Sooey cow," I yelled at the top of my voice and the Holsteins would come running to the barn. It was time for milking. I don't know whether they liked the sound of my voice or they were anxious for the molasses-topped ground grain. Every cow had an assigned spot in the barn and she always knew where to go. A stanchion kept her in place until the milking was finished.

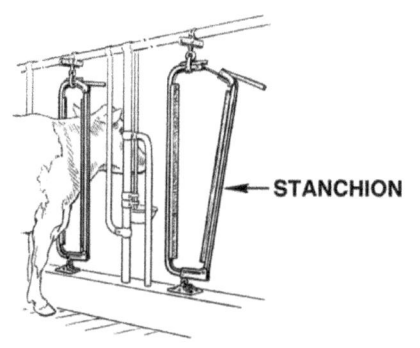

Every night and morning through the summer, either my brother Curt or I had to help with the milking. When school started, we were only on call during the evening. We traded off for a change of duty when an exciting option came our way, like going to a friend's house or a movie with a friend.

We were just glad that we were as old as we were. The previous generation had to do the milking by hand. Our farm was now equipped with electric milking machines. But our real gripe was that our school buddies played ball, went to the movies on Saturdays and slept in every summer day. When you grow up on a farm, you're expected to "earn your keep," as my Grandmother often reminded us.

One of our jobs was to wash each cow's udder before attaching the milking machine.

And this was such an important job, because the state inspector made random visits to check sanitation. If this examiner found a problem, he could prevent the sale of milk until he came back a week later to see if the situation was corrected. This could be devastating to a farmer. The lesson was to do a job well.

We also had to haul cow feed and carry buckets of milk to the milk cooler.

Besides milking, there was hay baling, combining grain and filling the silo. There was less barn work to do in the summer because the Holsteins spent most of their time in the pasture. Since the cows were only in the barn for milking, we didn't have to shovel manure, put down clean straw bedding or haul silage from the silo to the feeding troughs. My dad affectionately referred to hauling manure as "hauling out the dividends." I didn't know what he meant when I was a kid.

During the summer and weekend mornings, we really wanted to sleep in. We could almost hear reveille, as Dad called one of us from our sleep at 6 a.m. It was like the old army song lines, "Oh how I hate to get up in the morning, Oh how I'd love to stay in bed." Okay, Irving Berlin, I've heard enough.

I felt like I missed out on a lot of activities while I was growing up, but when I look back, I learned lessons that I would probably never have learned if I had grown up in town.

Dad often reminded me that a dairy was like a prison without bars. Do you think he was trying to tell me something?

Because of my early chores on the family farm, I learned what hard work could accomplish. I never thought that the "time with the cows" would be such valuable job training. It taught me the value of hard work and responsibility on a job. Every morning and evening, somebody had to be there.

"Milk. It Does a Body Good," was the slogan of the National Dairy Council in the 1980s. Who knew that it would be so good for my body and my life?

15. HOUSECLEANING, A RITE OF SPRING

Our house was located up a long curved driveway. Any looker would need binoculars to be able to gaze at us. No peeping Tom could ever look in our house. Each window had a window blind, most of which didn't roll up and down as they were supposed to, but that didn't matter. I tried to pull one down when the early morning sun appeared in my bedroom, only to spend time taking the blind down and rolling it up by hand. Tree-lined fields and meandering streams created "picture windows" in every direction – even the barn and out buildings bring to mind a picture-postcard of farm country. Who needed window blinds?

Drapes never adorned the ivory painted frames that surrounded the windows. Lace curtains were my mother's choice. The sheer panels that resembled tiny screen fabric hung at all the windows. Some curtains came with designs that looked like lace, while others were plain. Plenty of natural light brightened our farm house.

The standard coal furnace, affectionately known as "The Monster in the Basement," pumped out tons of heat to warm our family, and we could sit near a large vent to warm our feet after a winter day of working outside, or an afternoon of sled riding on many of the steep hills that surround the farm.

In addition to the cozy warmth that was forced into the six rooms, coal dust and soot came along for the ride. The coal dust settled on the floors, the furniture, the curtains as well as the walls and ceiling. It didn't discriminate. All the rooms were treated equally with each being coated in the gray shades that toned down the pale greens and wheat shades of the painted walls. I never noticed the dust collection during the heating season.

The Hoover, along with buckets of water, mops, dust cloths and corn brooms kept the floors and furniture spotless, but each spring, every room in the house had to be cleaned, from floor to ceiling. Coal dust had to be washed from the enamel painted walls—a labor intensive undertaking that required work on a step ladder to reach the highest parts. We used water with the pungent odor of Spic and Span and rags that had seen a former life as bath towels. Just apply elbow grease.

I never realized how dirty the painted surfaces were until I came from school one day and saw my mother reigning from the ladder, her subjects—the bucket, the rag and the enamel painted surfaces. The clean parts were no longer "dirty wheat." When she took a break, I climbed the ladder and tried my hand as a wall scrubber. I didn't reign as well as she did. The part that I washed was merely smeared. I kept my day job as a student—it was easier.

The upstairs bedrooms were another story (no pun intended). These rooms had wallpaper. This was before vinyl coated paper. But remember, there's no discrimination. These rooms were just as dirty, except that no water would ever touch the papered walls. They were cleaned with wall paper cleaner. It resembled Play-Doh, but had a minty smell.

The cleaning person took a glob of the cleaner in hand, much like a handful of bread dough and spread it over a small area of wallpaper. When removed from the wall, voila, the dirty surface was cleaned. A year's worth of dirt was transferred to the cleaning product. Knead the cleaner to mix the sooty surface into it and repeat the operation. One glob of cleaner could be used for a long time, but eventually absorbed too much dirt and had to be tossed out. No amount of kneading could produce a clean surface. (Incidentally, Play-Doh, as we know it today had its beginning as wall paper cleaner.)

With floors and walls of the house newly cleaned, Mom now turned to washing the lace curtains. Because of their delicate nature, they were washed in a large basin in the sink, using mild laundry soap. Because there was so much coal dust, they had to be rinsed twice. After they were thoroughly rinsed, she put them to dry on a curtain stretcher, outside in the sun.

If you've never met a curtain stretcher, it could be a scary finger destroyer for the younger family members. The curtain stretcher is a large adjustable wooden frame that could be sized according to the dimensions of the curtains. Brad-like nails that more nearly resembled straight pins projected from the edges of the wooden frame where they looked like tin soldiers marching around the edge of the frame, waiting to jag the fingers of children who weren't supposed to touch. The wet curtains, fresh from their rinsing were attached onto the frame with the pins projecting through them.

To avoid pierced fingers the human had to maneuver carefully as the wet curtains were attached to the drying frame.

"I don't want you kids touching the curtain stretchers. You'll hurt your fingers."

"Mom, I got blood on my finger and the curtains."

"I told you to keep your fingers away from there. Now I have to take the curtains off and wash the blood out."

"I was just trying to help."

The entire cleaning process changed radically in the early 1960s when we got a new gas-fired, hot water heating system. No more floor vents. Not as much dust and dirt. Mom still did the spring cleaning. It wasn't as intense, but the need to spring clean was in her DNA.

My Mother's Clean House

She mopped the floors and washed the walls,
She dusted the furniture and cleaned the halls.

Spic and Span™ was her product—the heavy grime remover,
But when it came to the carpets, she liked the upright Hoover.

The Good Housekeeping seal of approval must have been her goal,
But why'd she have to involve me? I think she was out of control.

16. THE MONSTER IN THE CELLAR

There's that noise again—bang, clang, screech—comin' from the cellar.
"What are those noises?" I asked my mother. "It sounds like a monster down there."
"Maybe it is," she told me.
I didn't know whether she was joking—sometimes she did that.
"I'm never going to go down there unless you go with me."
There wasn't much reason for me to go there, but her answer did cause some pause for question—after all, it was a cellar, not a basement.
I never thought about it in the summer but I still wouldn't go down alone until I said to myself, *There's no such thing as a monster living at our house. I'm going down by myself.*
I did go up and down ten times the day that I decided that monsters DIDN'T live in the cellar, but I still didn't like to go down there at night, just in case.
It turns out that the only monster in the cellar was the humongous coal/wood furnace that creaked when my Dad pulled the lever back and forth to sieve the ashes from the still burning coals. They screeched as they filtered through the grates in a fiery display or when a piece of wet log sizzled and hissed as the oozing sap squirted into the fire and cracked like a small Roman candle. Those were the noises that made the furnace seem like a monster. That monster ate huge amounts of coal and firewood and belched at times. This produced those piles and piles of ashes. The ashes were a great abrasive on a snowy driveway to get the 1941 Chevy and later the 1952 Chevy up the driveway when the snow packed down and formed a bed of ice. It was easier than putting chains on the car.
Mr. Coal Furnace really did look like a monster. Hot air ducts spread their tentacles out over the entire cellar ready to grab me before they delivered hot air to the upstairs. Another big pipe sucked cold air from the hallway and sent it off to the fiery chamber to be heated and recycled. I could have fit into that pipe easily. You know how it is with monster pipes, you can never be too careful.

Another big pipe was the one that collected the smoke from the furnace. It stretched across half the basement where it held on to the opening in the chimney. Black smoke looked like it was sending a signal as it rose up to the sky and floated away. That smoke pipe was about five feet off the floor. At one point, I had to start ducking to get under it—growth does that. My parents had always had to lower their heads to get under. But the best part is that it was covered with asbestos. One of my favorite things to do as a young one was to jump up and slap it as I passed under. Hello Mesothelioma. Welcome to my body.

Another scraping noise that the monster let out was the shovel dragging against the ash chamber as Dad scratched and dumped the ashes into an old grease bucket. Then I could hear another but different scrape as the coal shovel scuffed into the coal that was being loaded into the "The Monster." By the time I reached the age of understanding, I decided that "The Monster" could be an affectionate name from my childhood for this monstrosity that lived in the belly of our house. That's when I decided to call him Mr. Monster.

One of the other reasons Mr. Monster looked so at home in the cellar was because the floor was dirt. He looked like the monster that I had seen in the movie, "Creature from the Lost Lagoon," as he crept up from the mud soaked earth. The only concrete to be found in this cellar was that on which Mr. Monster sat. All through the Monsoon season the surrounding dirt floor became a swamp. Dad had to wear mukluks to go down there. It took days of an open window and cellar door to dry the swamp-like surface after the rains ended. During a house renovation project the cellar got a new concrete floor.

After workmen leveled the dirt in the cellar and poured the new floor the rain from the back porch drained into the cellar, ran across the slightly sloping floor and was sucked down a drain that ran to the lower yard. The cellar had almost become a basement, but not yet. That didn't happened until about five years later when Mr. Monster was replaced with two small furnaces, one which burned natural gas and the other that burned coal and wood. They were joined together by Dad's friend Mr. Simpson, who was a retired steamfitter. Hot water was heated in these furnaces and was pumped throughout the house to warm it like we had never known before. Mr. Monster had given space to these two small guys that were about one-fifth his size.

I now have pleasant memories of the amazing Mr. Monster, even though I don't miss him.

17. MOM, I'M HOME

There was never a year in my conscious memory of life with my mother that I remember her being well for 12 consecutive months. But when she was healthy, she was one of the most active, social and entertaining people I knew. Living on a farm and raising a family was her full time job. She was a natural cook, preparing organic meals long before organic was popular, since almost all the food was produced on the farm.

She fixed mainly foods that my dad liked. I asked her why I had to try something I didn't like, because when Dad doesn't like it, we don't eat it.

Sundays were open house—no invitation needed. Friends and relatives would drop in and there was always room for one or five more at the table.

Our kitchen counter held a green barrel shaped cookie jar—and it was almost always full. But if we tried to sneak a cookie out of it before supper, we would hear, "Stay out of that cookie jar. Supper's almost ready." She didn't really have eyes in the back of her head. The cookie jar lid squeaked when we tried to put it back on. We affectionately called it the no sneak cookie jar.

She baked twice a week until the Nickles Bakery truck started to deliver, so I could have my fix of doughy white bread. I was the only kid in first grade that brought sandwiches on homemade bread.

Since automation wasn't very prevalent in the 40s and 50s, she had a wringer Maytag washer and a clothes line. When I came from school, I could tell it was wash day because of the fresh-washed clothes smell that greeted me at the door. When automatic washers became popular, my mother refused to get one.

Our family had huge gardens which produced corn, beans, peas, potatoes, onions, carrots, broccoli, cucumbers, zucchini and tomatoes. The excess had to be prepared for canning or freezing. My mom even canned meat when my dad butchered pigs.

The Rhode Island Reds provided extra cash for her. She fed them and gathered the eggs and although my dad raised and ground the chicken feed, my mother got the cash from the sale of eggs and dressed chickens. This was her money, which she kept in an aluminum cup that sat on the top shelf of the Hoosier cabinet. Even though it was supposed to be her money, she used a big part of it to pay for my college tuition and music lessons.

Everything that was done on the farm seemed to be labor intensive—preserving food, washing clothes, cleaning the house, preparing meals and maintaining the area around the house. I can remember my mother saying that she was tired, but she still had work to do. She would spend the evenings in the living room where she embroidered linen dresser scarves and pillows and edged them with lace. Other evenings she patched my jeans which often had holes in the knees.

She taught me how to work. At the end of the day, her question often was, "What do you have to show for the day?" She and my father were role models for hard work.

One of my favorite Saturday night things was to poke through the stores in Canonsburg with her while my dad played pool. We often stopped at Jeffrey's Drug Store for ice cream.

Mothers are supposed to be your best friend and my mother was mine. She took great care of me and taught me how to treat people. She tried to show me right from wrong. I should have listened to her. I never heard her swear. The only time I heard her use an off color word, she spelled it. She was quoting some else's conversation. Mom was devoted to her family. Membership in the Presbyterian Church sustained her strong faith, and God's word was a particular source of strength and hope for her.

"Mom, I'm home. Where are you?" I sing-songed as I came into the kitchen after school.

She didn't answer.

"Mom, where are you?" I repeated.

I heard some faint words from her upstairs bedroom. "I'm not myself."

Then I surveyed the kitchen. The day's dishes were still in the sink and the daily paper and mail were still lying on the corner of the dining room table. I knew it was the beginning of a different way of life at our house. It would last a few months. It always had.

Mom had a medical condition known as depression. That's the term I heard so often when I was a kid. I really didn't know what it meant, early on, but I knew that part of the time my Mother withdrew from her daily activities and either stayed in bed or stretched out on the living room couch. When she was depressed she didn't do any work. She didn't entertain. She didn't shop. She didn't visit people. She didn't go to church or social activities, and other people seldom came to visit.

"How's your mother?" was the question I heard so often. Everybody—many relatives and the neighbors knew that Mom had this problem. I hated the question, because when she was depressed, I had to say that she was not her lively self. I didn't like the responses from the people who asked about her. Everyone seemed to have an idea as to what she should do to get better.

"She should take Vitamin B."

"She should see Dr. Cure-all or Dr. He-can-help. They helped my neighbor who was like your mother."

"Did she ever take Brewer's Yeast? It's supposed to cure depression. Maybe that what's she needs."

"She should see Dr. Twigg. He's an (American) Indian doctor from Fayette County. He prepares his own medicines. He kept my sister alive."

"Dr. Downey can give her a B-12 shot. That should help her."

Everybody had a suggestion for what could solve my mother's illness, but nobody else had to deal with her condition.

Nobody's suggestion worked. I heard my dad tell someone that he'd spent a small fortune on doctors, some of whom I believe were quacks.

In the early years, I never really understood the situation. I didn't know why my mother couldn't get up, do her usual chores or function like she did when she was in her manic state. That was the medical term for the time when she was high.

In addition to the sessions with local general practitioners, mom had sessions with psychiatrists. When I was in tenth grade, she spent a period of time at St. Francis Hospital in Pittsburgh. After several office sessions with her shrink, he suggested that she undergo shock therapy. Curt and I didn't see her for nearly a month. She did undergo the treatments while she was a patient at the hospital. When I asked my dad about her condition, he said, "She won't be the same when she comes home." This was probably the only time that I had great concern for her health, because in my short time of dealing with her mental illness, she always recovered, sooner or later. From my dad's comments, I didn't know what to expect when she returned home.

She came home near her birthday in March, but I didn't see any difference in her personality. She had been depressed when she entered the hospital, but came home feeling well. It didn't last though. She eventually cycled back to the depressed state. I could never identify a time of year—summer, winter, spring or fall—when the melancholy was more prominent. It seemed to have its phases, and the positive state eventually returned.

Another time Dad, Curt and I met with the psychiatrist from the local hospital's mental health ward. I don't think the doctor really knew or understood my mom. She was worried about Mom killing herself. After the meeting, Mom asked me, "Did she say something about me killing myself? Why do they always think I want to kill myself? Don't they know I just want to get better?" I don't think my mother was ever suicidal.

The best thing about the time at the local hospital was a woman she met while there. Her name was Effie. They became friends and shopped together, visited others and generally had a good time. I don't remember what Effie's problem was. Her southern roots and sense of humor became a good influence on my mother. One day Effie and Mom were on their way to town when Effie's Cadillac stalled in a busy traffic intersection. The man in the car behind laid on his horn. After about the third time he honked, Effie got out of her car and went back to talk with the distressed man.

"I'd be glad to sit in your car and lay on the horn if you got in my car and started it," Effie told him. Effie got back in her car, and eventually it started.

Effie came to visit often. She tried to counsel Mom to good health, but curing depression takes more than talk. Effie was not the first who tried to talk Mom back to health. Although friends were great advisors, they could not change the landscape of depression. Mainly they came and brought food.

At times, my Grandmother Neill helped with the housework and cooking. But, she often stayed with her sister for extended periods of time. She was getting older and not always in good health to keep a house in order. Dad hired neighbors and relatives to come and help out. Sometimes these people cooked. After all the good cooking we were used to, we often had canned soup and a sandwich.

Out of all this, some good did happen. I learned how to cook. Even if my mother was lying around the house, I could ask her how to prepare a certain food. Her response often was, "I don't want to talk about food." It seems that when she was dealing with a bout of depression, food didn't interest her, and she didn't want to talk about it. With a little questioning I learned that I could get the information that I needed.

I also learned to wash clothes using the wringer washer—whites, brights and darks.

I don't think my mother's depression should define her life because when she was not depressed she took off like a hamster on a treadmill. She got more work done than most farm wives. But when she slipped into depression, life at our house changed. The darker times of mom's sadness are repressed in my adult memory. I think time glosses over the things I don't like to remember. I tend to see her as a loving caring mother—a woman who lived a great life in spite of the down times.

Most of the neighbors and relatives didn't understand this branch of mental illness. Barbara Kingsolver expresses this well in The Bean Tree: "There is no point in treating a depressed person as though she were just feeling sad, saying, 'There now, hang on, you'll get over it.' Sadness is more or less like a head cold—with patience it passes. Depression is like cancer."

18. CONES, KLONDIKES AND THE ICE CREAM MAN

I don't know whether it was a curse or I was lucky, but I've always liked sweets, especially ice cream. When I was young, a Sunday drive regularly seemed to end up going past an ice cream shop, and we often stopped to get a cone. I can still see the melting chocolate running down onto my hand. "Lick your hand," Dad instructed.

One of my favorite stops was a shop that was built in the shape of an inverted cone. A little door folded up to the inside and created a small counter from which the "dipper" dipped one's favorite flavor. The other preferred location was Isaly's[4] where the specialty was the "Skyscraper Cone." It was at least seven inches tall. I never got this because it was too much to eat. I got the five-cent cone that was about the size of half a tennis ball. Sometimes I got a foil wrapped chocolate dipped square of ice cream called a "Klondike," usually the one with crispy rice.

I remember getting a Nutty Buddy at a wayside market. I was too young to realize that it was well on its way to melting when I selected it. I loved the solid, rich chocolate which wrapped around the luscious vanilla ice cream, all this encased in a cake cone, topped with nuts. Before we drove away the sweet concoction was running down onto my hand, so I bit off the bottom of the cone thinking I could stop the dripping. NOT! Then the melting ice cream started dripping out the bottom of the cone as well.

The ice cream we had at home was made using the hand turned freezer or it was bought from a place that would pack it in dry ice. The dry ice kept it cold for several hours. Ice cream in dry ice was often a treat at school picnics, family reunions and birthday parties.

Of course this all happened before we had a freezer at home in which to store ice cream. Our old Frigidaire refrigerator had a freezer compartment large enough for six ice cube trays. We kept two trays. We had always

---

[4] We remembered how to spell Isaly's: I Shall Always Love You Sweetheart.

rented a frozen food locker at the Washington Ice Company. Each week we brought home some frozen meat and vegetables that we had grown and stored there. We usually had a couple packages of beef and vegetables like corn or peas. These had to be used during the week since this freezer didn't stay as cold as the one at the ice house. Then we'd bring home more next week.

In the early 1950s we got a 23-cubic-foot Revco deep freezer which held about twenty times as much as our old ice box freezer. This nearly ten-foot-long freezer took up a large portion of the basement. It sort of resembled a huge steamer trunk with double lids. This new appliance radically changed the ice cream eating habits of our family.

I don't know how he knew, but Mr. Snee, who drove an ice cream delivery truck started coming to our house. All the neighborhood kids called him "The Ice Cream Man." Now the ice cream shop came to our back door.

Mr. Snee knew that Friday near lunch time was a good time to stop, especially in summer. Kids are great impulse buyers; they pester their parents until they give in and buy what the kid wants. (Some things never change.) Mr. Snee carried the usual ice cream treats like Eskimo Pies, Nutty Buddies, Popsicles, Dreamsicles and ice cream sandwiches. In addition, there were half gallons and for the big appetite, Mr. Snee had two-and-a-half-gallon containers of selected varieties like chocolate ripple, butter pecan, White House, vanilla and Neapolitan.

After the freezer came to live in the basement, we still stopped for ice cream at places like the Dairy Queen, but most of the time we ate ice cream at home. My Gram used to say, "There's nothing wrong with me a little ice cream won't fix." I had to agree with her. I still do.

19. HOME MADE ICE CREAM

Sometimes we got our ice cream at Isaly's or a local shop. Sometimes Mr. Snee, "the Ice Cream Man," delivered it to our house. But sometimes on hot summer evenings or lazy Sunday afternoons my brother and I would beg our parents to let us make ice cream. After all, we lived on a dairy farm and always had the ingredients for this frozen treat.

Little did we realize that our parents used this request to their advantage. They got us to do a lot of chores without any argument. Feed the chickens. Gather the eggs. Clean the cow manure out of the barn. . .

When I studied education, the professor talked about the Premack principle – reward a positive behavior with a desired reinforcement and you're likely to get the desired result the next time. We certainly got what we wanted and that was ice cream. Curt and I did all these requested chores without being asked twice.

After our parents finally ran out of jobs for us to do, we were then allowed to get the old wooden ice cream freezer that lived on a shelf in the cellar behind the *Monster*. Curt and I would argue over who was going to get the freezer. Almost always we ended up going to the cellar together, especially if it was night time, because there was safety in numbers.

Our old ice cream freezer could produce one quart of ice cream, but that was enough for the five people who lived in our house. Although our freezer was old, the hand-cranked ice cream churn had been invented in 1846 by Nancy Johnson. That's when ice cream surged in popularity. Our original wooden freezer looked like it might have been one of the first. Eventually it rotted and we got a new plastic one.

Salt is essential in making hand cranked ice cream. My Dad bought it in a 50-pound bag for animal use. When the new bag was opened at the barn, a big bowl was filled for the kitchen use. But on this day, we brought a large metal dipper full to use in the ice cream machine.

One of the main ingredients of our recipe was cream. We had lots of cream. Since the milk was not processed, the cream rose to the top of the storage tank. Our job, before making ice cream, was to skim the fresh cream from the top of the milk.

We made this ice cream many times during the year, but it actually should be called frozen custard because the recipe includes eggs in addition to cream and sugar. Ice cream without eggs is called ice cream; most people still refer to the egg mixture as "ice cream."

The summer after we got the freezer it was easy to make our favorite dessert. We just saved up enough ice cubes to fill the ice cream freezer, while in the winter we'd bring in the packed snow and keep packing it in the space between the canister and the wooden bucket.

Fill the canister with the ice cream mixture. Place the canister in the bucket and put the crank on the top where it is locked into place with a wing-nut like device. After the freezer parts are all in place the space between the canister and the freezer is filled with ice. This is only the beginning. The handle could be turned for days and the mixture will not freeze. This is where science comes to bear. It is necessary to add salt to the ice to start the process of freezing the mixture.

What does the salt do?

Just like we use salt on icy roads in the winter, salt mixes with ice and causes the ice to melt. When salt comes into contact with ice, the freezing point of the ice is lowered. Water will normally freeze at 32 degrees F. A 10 percent salt solution freezes at 20 degrees F, and a 20 percent solution freezes at 2 degrees F. By lowering the temperature at which ice is frozen, we are able to create an environment in which the milk mixture can freeze into ice cream at a temperature below 32 degrees F. It takes about a half hour to convert the liquid mixture to ice cream. The rotating canister transfers the cold to the liquid mixture and that's how it freezes.

Our family liked vanilla, but there are many alternatives available for this process. Our other favorites were any kind of fruit and chocolate.

I never realized how often I would use the ice cream project until I started teaching. When I taught in the elementary school, holidays were celebrated with a party. The upper age level kids didn't always like the children's party. As a change of pace, one time during the year, usually Valentine's Day, the party was still held, but ice cream making was added as the main aspect and a science lesson.

Each student got to turn the handle of the ice cream freezer. Each had an opportunity to add salt to the ice. Each had a chance to see how the ingredients are mixed together and converted from the liquid mixture to the solid ice cream.

Electric ice cream freezers are available and many people use them. However, it is still fun to turn the freezer by hand to observe the process. I attended a family function recently were the ice cream freezer was operated by turning the freezer with a steam engine. It really took the process back in history to a time when wood was used to heat water and turn it into steam to turn an axle which drives a belt and turns the freezer with ease.

Ice cream wasn't just a mouthwatering treat anymore. It had become a valuable teaching tool and one that also was rewarded with a mouthwatering incentive. Now we make it with the grand-children. It's still a valued experience and motivation.

Frozen Custard Recipe

4 eggs	2 ½ cups of sugar
Approximate 5 cups of milk	4 cups cream
2 tablespoons of vanilla	¼ teaspoon of salt

Directions:

In a large heavy saucepan, bring milk to a boil. Meanwhile combine the sugar salt and eggs. Gradually add a small amount of milk to the egg mixture. Return all to the saucepan. Cook and stir until the mixture reaches at least 160 degrees F. and coats the back of a metal spoon. Add the cream and vanilla.

Chill for three to four hours.

Fill the canister of the freezer two thirds full. Freeze according to manufacturer's directions.

20. LIFE IN BLACK AND WHITE

Life in the early 1950s in Washington County, Pennsylvania, was mainly black and white. Movies were black and white. The neighbor's TV was black and white. Even the cows were black and white. Most of the cats that people dropped off at our farm were black and white. At one time we had 27 cats. The census was similar to the cows. You'd have thought our farm was part of the Humane Society. Some cat donors just left their unwanted felines at the end of our road. We welcomed these exterminators; they worked for food.

Why did we keep so many cats? Because we had mice and rats looking for free housing in the granary of the barn and the corn crib. Not only did the vermin wish to share the living spaces, they wanted to share in the food that was reserved for the farm animals. For them it was like an "all you can eat buffet," open all the time with many choices.

All our cats drank fresh milk that was poured into an old cake pan in the barn. They supplemented their diet with their honed hunting skills. After all, my dad had hired them for their pest control abilities.

The cats had built-in radar to know when the cows came into the barn. Pavlov's dogs had nothing on our cats. They salivated at six in the morning and six in the evening. Hungry cats waited at the milking area for their next liquid meal to appear. They didn't even hear a bell. During the day, they headed out into the fields that surrounded the farm buildings, preying on the pests. Maybe it was the old adage that the mouse is tastier on the other side of the fence.

Many days I stayed in the barn and helped Dad with the chores. But on this particular day, the crabs in the shallow Goose Creek were calling me. The Chartiers Creek at the other end of the farm was deeper than I liked for crabbing.

It was a great escape on a sunny day, away from baling hay or work in the barn. There were also scads of minnows swimming away from the intrusion of the small stream fisherman, too fast for a novice to catch.

I was intent on locating all the crabs I could find to put in a discarded pickle jar. Collecting crabs with an old kitchen sieve was a great way to spend an afternoon. Eventually that stream lost its plant and animal life because of a chemical plant about three miles upstream that washed pollutants into the stream. The animal medicine by-products manufactured at the factory were not friendly to the stream animals and the large crops of watercress that grew along the stream.[5] Crabbing was a good gig for Curt and me while it lasted.

On this particular afternoon, I didn't know my favorite black and white cat had followed me to the crabbing site. It had never happened before. Watching him carefully, I continued my small stream search for the best crustaceans available. They'd probably just deteriorate in the jar on the back porch, but it was part of the summer fun.

Most of the 27 cats didn't have names, so when I waded bare foot, out of the water, I headed toward one of my favorite felines and called, "Here Kitty, Here Kitty."

But Kitty didn't come to me as he always had. He just went in the opposite direction. *Maybe he's on the trail of a mole or a field mouse.*

This black and white animal wasn't friendly with me as I tried to catch and pet him among the skunk cabbage and iron weeds. It was at about this time my nose that this wasn't Kitty, but an imposter. *Now what am I going to do?* It was a cat all right, but this was what Gram called a "pole" cat. This black and white skunk used the only defense that it had to protect itself. Then it hit me; not the skunk's spray, but the idea that the skunk's defense permeated the area, me and my clothes. I had been skunked.

I had smelled a skunk's defense as we drove by a dead carcass along our country road, but had never been this close to experience the skunk's protection. I was defenseless.

"Oh no," I shrieked as I realized what was going on. "I'm in trouble now."

All of a sudden the pickle jar, loaded with precious small stream cargo was forgotten as this fisherman headed toward home port, on dry land.

I walked through the back door to where my mom was washing dishes in the kitchen.

"Get out of here," she yelled. "You stink like a skunk."

"Where'll I go?"

"Get to the shower in the cellar, and shower for several minutes, with lots of soap."

After I showered and changed clothes, I came to the kitchen with my dirty clothes.

"Get those skunk-stenched clothes out of my kitchen."

---

5   The chemical plant is long gone and life has now returned to the Goose Creek. When I was a kid, no laws were in place to protect the environment.

"What should I do with them?"

"Throw them away. Take them to the dump behind the barn."

"But they're my favorites."

"Take them to the dump."

"Do I have to?"

"Take them to the dump. I'm not telling you again," she said.

And the dump is where they went. They weren't my favorite shorts and tee-shirt any longer.

Oh well, they probably will be too small by next year.

What was it like growing up in black and white? It was the greatest, except for one day.

21. MAID IN THE SHADE

As long as I can remember my Gram Myers' hair was always in a tight twisted bun at the back of her head. Imagine my surprise when I walked into the kitchen to find her standing in front of the mirror with her long peppered gray hair spread across her shoulders and traveling halfway down her back.

"Gram, are you going to wear a pony tail?"

"I don't know what you're talking about."

Indeed, ponytail was not a word in Gram's vocabulary. She'd never been to a beauty shop and didn't know what it was like to have a stylist cut her hair—after all her sister always trimmed it. No hair dryer ever got near her head. She just let it air dry, then twisted it into a long rope and coiled it into a bun, which was held in place with the tortoise colored hair pins.

On many afternoons, we could hear the pleasant sing-song as she glided back and forth next to the kitchen window. The tan patterned linoleum showed the worn tracks from many years of the traveling rocker.

As she peered out the side window, she had a view of the world along Mingo Creek. She could see the changing of the seasons as the trees turned from green to gold, red and orange in the fall. She, the good farmer, predicted the weather by observing the sky and cloud formations. She had a very good record of weather prediction at a time when weather forecasting was done by reading sky signs. I remember her saying that clouds going in different directions (e.g. one layer going west, another layer going north) means bad weather is coming. Another formation that she called the "mare's tail" was really Cirrus clouds. I later learned they are high in the sky like long streamers. They mean bad weather within the next 36 hours. But her favorite was "Red sky at night, Sailor's delight. Red sky in the morning, Sailors take warning." And sure enough, that's what the weather often did.

This window on the world allowed her to keep track of the comings and goings of the milk cows and the work horses as they drank from an old clawfoot bathtub that served as a watering trough. The pigs were in view where they squealed and pushed to share the same gems as they rooted in the sod. She could even know when the neighbors, the only other family along the road, passed by. Although the window was her constant lookout on the world, she still worked on hand sewing, embroidery and quilting from the best seat in the house. It was also her hair drying seat.

In the summer, she moved to the front porch of the brown Insulbrick house. Two blue swings, each with a quilted pad that she had made, faced from opposite ends of the gray porch. It became the "summer" center of family fun, and relaxation. Where else could you sit and swing yourself to sleep or read the Sunday afternoon away? It was a great cool, shady escape from the heat of the kitchen. It was the main summer meeting place when the rest of the family visited.

My grandfather, her husband, died in 1925, three days after he had contracted the flu. Gram and my Uncle Ross, who was 15 at the time, continued to work the farm. Many days of working with horses in the fields and tilling a garden left her with brown wrinkled skin that never came in contact with Coppertone. A vintage sun bonnet shaded her high forehead and eyes. No sunglasses for this hard worker.

She always reminded her grandchildren that hard work never hurt anyone. If you look up "hard work" in the family dictionary, you'll see her picture. Her weathered skin and her work ethic made her a "no nonsense" Grandmother. Her rough hands with leather glove like fingers, from outdoor work still didn't deter her from the duties of feeding hungry faces. I don't know how she did everything. There were always good treats when we went to her house like tapioca pudding, raisin cookies and homemade ice cream in the summer.

Preparing food at her house wasn't easy. There was no electricity until 1948, nor was there running water; indirectly there was, but it came from a pipe that connected to a hillside spring. This pipe was attached to the faucet of the modern kitchen sink and ran continually—you couldn't close or plug up the drain. If you wanted hot water, you had to fill the large tea kettle and place it on the coal stove. Even with the lack of kitchen appliances, she was able to produce some of the most tasty pastries, candies and puddings. I loved her pies and cookies.

Since there was no electricity on this farm, there were no electric milking machines. Gram got up with the cows and she and Uncle Ross hand milked twenty cows. She would put on her work dress and hike up the hill to the barn. No pants for this lady. "Pants are for men," she always said. Of course there were large aprons to cover the dresses worn in the house—granny prints for my Gram. They were made from old feed sacks.

Gram greeted the cows as they came from the pasture in the summer and as they awakened in the barn during winter. She and Uncle Ross each milked their ten favorite cows every morning and evening. The cows like pets, had names and she talked to them as each found their spot in the barn.

Gram had never flipped the pages of *Glamour* or read a *Women's Wear Daily*, but she always dressed up for special occasions. Sunday dresses came from J.C. Penney or Caldwell's in Washington, Pennsylvania. She didn't care for flowered prints on her Sunday dresses—solid dark blue, maroon or dark green dresses were all in her wardrobe, but they were always adorned with a fancy brooch, often in the shape of flowers. Maybe she wanted to be "plain Jane," after all that was her middle name. A hat was a necessity to wear to church. How about a navy blue straw with matching ribbon and small feather?

It was hard to tell that this farmer, manager, cook, mother and grandmother had worked the day before in the field or had prepared food for the family who might show up after church. She wasn't a fashion plate, but did enjoy dress-up clothes on the Sabbath as she always called it.

When I stayed at her house in the early 1950s, she had stopped doing so much farm work, but still liked to work in the garden. I was ten years old.

"Come along," she invited. "We're going to hoe some rows of corn." She gathered her bonnet and headed to the shed behind the house to pick up the tools.

"Do I have to?" I asked her, "I have to do that at home. I thought I was on vacation."

"You are on vacation, but there's still work to do."

So off we went to cut the choking weeds that tend to strangle out the young corn stalks. I was all excited when we finished the corn, but then she directed me to the rows of green beans to continue with the removal of weeds and stir the dirt around the plants to nurture them. After finishing the tidying of the vegetable plants, we had to pick the early garden peas, which we'd eat for lunch. Who knew that she already had a meatloaf and potatoes baking in the oven?

It was a memorable dinner, but they all were (farmers called the noon meal dinner). After eating, there was no rest.

"Let's go," she said, "We're going out to the cow pasture to cut weeds."

"What?"

"We're not done yet. Those weeds behind the chicken house need to be cut."

Gee whiz, maybe I should have stayed at home.

Maybe that's why I saw her head bobbing a little as she sat in her rocker in the late afternoon. She worked from sun rise to sunset.

In her later years, Gram moved around, living with our family and each of her other children. Her children's homes were her personal care home. When she came to our house, my brother Curt and I nicknamed her The Maid. We thought that she was our maid. She still held onto the work ethic. She helped my mother by peeling potatoes, cleaning green beans or washing dishes. She also got into repairing ripped blue jeans, sewing on buttons and sewing quilt patches—and then she asked, "What else do you have for me to do?"

She even sat on our back porch, in the shade and continued working. She was our "maid in the shade."

I never heard her say, "I'm bored."

22. THE FORBIDDEN ROOM

The parlor was the mysterious room at my grandmother's house that was off limits to a five-year-old boy, but I could peek in as I went upstairs. The big dark brown overstuffed sofa and chairs looked so inviting. I would have rather slept on them than on my bed. My grandmother was forever crocheting little doilies that always ended up on the parlor furniture, to help protect the backs and arms. I later learned that they are called antimacassars. Other than the upholstered furniture, there was pattern everywhere. Great big cabbage roses in shades of dark rose and blue-gray adorned the walls. This was an invitation to take my crayons and shade in the roses. The carpet had ovals, triangles, curlicues and rectangles. What a construction site for my toy trucks and cars. It could have been a kid's indoor playground long before McDonalds.

On the far wall was a fireplace that was no longer a fireplace but held a small gas stove, the kind that holds porcelain columns which become orange when they're heated. Above this was a color tinted, sepia picture of Grandpap and his four brothers, in a curved glass frame. I always wondered why these guys were wearing suits when they were standing out among the apple trees on the farm. Any time I ever saw them out in the fields, there were wearing overalls.

The room was light and airy. The window treatments were lacy sheer curtains that allowed plenty of light to come into the room, but provided some privacy.

Every time my family went to visit Gram, we just sat around in the kitchen, the living room or the front porch in summer. I could have spent valuable time, alone in that sacred room, the parlor.

My day was coming. Aunt Hazel and Uncle Carl were going to get married, in the parlor. There was such frenzy. Uncle Ross borrowed folded chairs from the church so that all 30 guests could have a seat. The women were in the kitchen preparing light refreshments. And my 14-year-old cousin Doris was in the parlor, practicing her solo for the wedding, accompanied by Betty Jane Martin, Aunt Hazel's good friend. Usually Doris was in the parlor practicing piano. "Maybe if I take piano lessons, I'll get to go in the parlor to practice too."

On the day of the wedding when people arrived they were ushered into the parlor. Since my mother and dad were part of the wedding party, I had to sit next to my mother's cousin Paula, so she could keep an eye on me. She was an elementary teacher, and I was a handful. Well, I finally made it into the parlor, with 30 other people. I couldn't even see the construction site on the floor and I couldn't get near the couch. It and the chairs had been moved across the road to the garage.

It wasn't until my Uncle Ross gave me a ride in the milk truck, and dropped me off to visit Gram, that I finally got into the parlor, alone. Gram was working in the garden and didn't know that I had snuck into the house and headed straight for the parlor. Darn, I didn't even have my trucks or crayons with me, but I did lie on the couch.

23. QUILTING: AN ART

When I think about an artist, I don't think about my grandmother or my Great aunts. I think of someone in a smock sitting at an easel, but my Grandmother Neill and my Great Aunts Grace and Sarah were needle artists. They all wore house dresses and black, laced oxfords with a slight heel. All their glasses were frameless bifocals with wire temples. They all pulled their hair back and held it in place with side combs. No smocks for these ladies.

While they quilted, they talked and talked and gossiped. They sounded like third graders.

"Did you taste Belle's apple pie?"

"You mean the one that tasted like cardboard?"

"And how about that dress she was wearing? It looked like a little girl's first sewing project."

"She'd better find another line of work."

That's how it went. I never really heard them fight; they just bickered a little bit. And they did have reasons to squabble—politics. Aunt Sarah Donley had married a Republican, and Aunt Grace Carson married Walter, who had a prominent position in the Washington County Democratic Party. He had been the Prothonotary and a member of the Pennsylvania House of Representatives.

But artists they were, with needles. Each was an accomplished seamstress, as their mother had been. Their mother made a living by making dresses for other people. Each made their own "house dresses." Each crocheted, and each quilted. Gram Neill even did knitting.

One of my jobs was to crawl under the quilting frame to pick up the dropped threads. I did it once with the upright vacuum cleaner and then spent an hour picking with a pair of pliers and pulling the threads from the beater. Picking threads was my assigned job, but I was more interested in moving my toy trucks along the geometric designs of the parlor carpet. These carpet edge roads were obstructed by my Grandmother's black oxfords, and on this day a major traffic jam was created because there were more shoes blocking the "under quilt Interstate." My Great Aunts' shoes added to this kid's traffic snarls. A handful of threads didn't make much of a hill for my roadway.

After a day of quilting, the great aunts drove off to Scenery Hill in Aunt Grace's 1948 Ford Coupe. Gram said, "If you want something done right, you have to do it yourself."

She almost mumbled as she said it so I asked her what she meant. She didn't answer.

So, I asked my mom. Mom said their stitches weren't uniform and Gram would probably replace them. I figured that's why Mom never quilted on Gram's masterpieces. I got the idea that she was a perfectionist, even though I didn't know that word yet.

Gram's stitches were faultless—each was the same length like they had been done with a sewing machine that had a gauge at ten stitches per inch. Hers were always uniform and she expected the same from any quilter who joined her—especially her sisters.

All of Gram's quilt patches were handmade. She used a template made of sandpaper that she traced on a plywood lapboard before cutting the pieces and sewing them together into blocks by hand. She did all this while she sat in her overstuffed wing chair listening to the radio. She did get a little modern when she assembled the hand sewn patches together on her New Home electrified sewing machine—it had been a treadle operated machine, before it was converted.

Gram's quilts were works of art. Each of her seven grandchildren inherited a handmade quilt. Mine is large enough to fit a king size bed. Sometime she made an appliquéd quilt, but most of the time, she used a nine patch in many different variations. My brother's was assembled in shades of dark blue and white while mine is brown, orange, rust and white.

I also inherited a quilt that Great Grandmother Washabaugh had made. It was the Blue Ribbon winner at the 1925 Washington County Fair. It's a Wagon wheel pattern. I even have the blue ribbon.

Artists use different genres and different media. It just happens that the elder matriarchs in my family used needles and thread as their chosen medium.

The quilts that I have are a great remembrance of a Grandmother, who grew up in a time when women had to march to the tune of homemaking. She had a degree in elementary education but had to resign her position when she got married. I thought that all grandmas did needle arts, but eventually learned that few had the high level skill that she enjoyed.

24. A MEMORABLE CHRISTMAS

It looked like it was going to be a slim Christmas at our house. My mom was not feeling well. There were no decorations, no cookies and no sign of a Christmas tree. It was only three days till Christmas. I was probably 12 years old. Bah, humbug.

"Dad, are we getting a tree this year?" I asked impatiently. We'd never not had a Christmas tree.

"I haven't had time to get to town to get one," he answered me curtly.

"Okay."

It didn't even look like we'd have a big meal like we'd always had. My aunts and uncles and Gram were all going to someone else's Christmas meal. They'd all been at our house the year before.

Then it started to fall into place. Two days before Christmas, dad came home with a tree.

"Where'd you find *that* tree?" Curt asked. His voice showing disapproval.

"It's the only tree they had left on the lot."

Dad went back to the car to get some groceries and other stuff that he had bought.

"This tree looks like a big shrub," Curt said to me.

"I know. I guess it's better than none. It could be a Charlie Brown tree."

We got the tree holder and the decorations from the extra bedroom closet. It started with the light check. They were the type that if one bulb didn't work, none of them worked. It only took a half hour to get all the lights working. All the lights in the window candelabra worked, so that became our testing spot—one bulb at a time.

Curt draped the lights on the tree and asked if they were spaced correctly.

"I think so," I told him.

"Stand back and squint your eyes. The blank spots will jump out at you," he told me.

Then he added the bubble lights; they looked like small glass candles, with liquid inside. Small bubbles rose to the top as they heated up.

"They look great."

Next we added the fragile glass ornaments that had been around since dad was a kid.

"It's looking pretty good."

Next came the icicles. Curt didn't like the way I threw handfuls at the tree. I was dismissed from this part of the decorating.

I started supper while Curt finished his job. When I came back to the edge of the living room I told him it was a work of art. It didn't look like a Charlie Brown Christmas tree.

We still didn't know what we'd do for Christmas dinner.

On Christmas morning, we opened some games, new socks, flannel shirts and a new sled. We had cornflakes for breakfast, but there was no sign of a Christmas meal. It looked like we'd have sandwiches. There was no turkey or ham roasting in the oven. I asked Dad what we were going to eat.

"Maybe we'll have grilled cheese," he grumbled. I got the feeling that he was messing with our heads.

Then we got a call. Miss Alice, a church lady, was calling to tell us that she was bringing our Christmas dinner. Really, she was bringing a large roasted chicken, with stuffing and dessert. We added green beans and mashed potatoes. Mom rose from her bed and joined us for family Christmas dinner. Our Christmas turned out to be memorable.

I never realized the great responsibility my dad had to take care of farm, house and kids. He certainly was a trooper.

25. WASHINGTON COUNTY FAIR, 1954

"Let's go to the fair tonight, Dad!"
No answer.
"When can we go to the fair, dad?" I kept hassling.
"We don't go to the fair at night."
"When will we go?"
"We'll go on Thursday, all day."

When I was a kid, the county fair was the summer activity that farm kids dreamed of. We got to spend a day away from the daily grind of farm work. Adults probably felt the same way. We arrived around ten in the morning and stayed till four. We had to get home to tend the cattle in the evening. My brother Curt and I had to tag along with dad, which was a real bore. Dad didn't go to the fair to look at the exhibits. He went to talk with friends and neighbors.

I remember saying, "Dad, let's go look at the carnival."
"We'll go soon."

But most of the day, I spent waiting until he finished talking. When mom went, she walked the fairgrounds with me. But I was reaching the age that I didn't want to be seen tagging along on my mother's apron string.

When I was eleven, I was permitted to traipse around the grounds by myself. This was a newfound freedom. I just had to check in with dad every two hours. I looked in the exhibit hall at displays of fruits and vegetables, at the Grange and church presentations. I spent little time looking at the animals. I had plenty of animals to look at back home. I did check into the animal barns to see if any of my friends had won a blue ribbon for showing their prized animals. My family didn't take any animals to the fair. I kind of wished we had because the young people got to sleep in the empty stalls near their animal.

Dad gave me two dollars to spend for the day. Off I went to the carnival area where rows of games vied for my two dollars. Curt got the same amount, but he went with school friends.

"Throw the ball. Upset the milk bottles. Win a stuffed bear!" the man called to me.

I walked on. After all, it cost 20 cents.

"Grab a duck, win a prize," the next guy yelled.

This was a real temptation. It didn't take any skill like the milk bottle game. But there were more games to check out before parting with 20 cents.

My stomach tugged on my two dollars, so I surveyed the food stands. The carnival operated theirs out of trailers, while the churches and Granges had permanent buildings on the grounds. After a half-hour walk, I decided on a fish sandwich for 25 cents from our neighbor's church and a milkshake, made by the 4-H kids for 25 cents. Wow! I still have $1.50. Dad knew what he was doing. I had to shop and find the best use of two dollars.

Oops, I forgot to check in with dad. When I went to the meeting place, I couldn't see him.

"Dad, where are you?" I asked.

"Here I am."

Dad was still talking to the Allis Chalmers tractor dealer. He didn't realize that I had missed my check-in time.

As I started back to the midway, I met Great Aunt Sarah and Great Uncle Everett. They were sitting in the pavilion, eating the food that Aunt Sarah had prepared at home. It probably didn't cost them two dollars.

"Where are you going?" Aunt Sarah queried. "I'm on my way to check out the rides and the games. I already walked around once."

"Don't let the fakers take your money," Uncle Everett warned me.

"Who are the fakers?" I asked him.

"They're the guys who take your money; they run the games. They'll cheat you every time."

I decided to save my money after another trip around the carnival area. The guy who picked up a duck won a drinking glass, made of glass. If I won, I'd have to carry it. So, it was another jaunt around the food booths. French fries in a cone shaped cup and a cola set me back another 35 cents.

Then I saw the Ferris wheel. I wanted to ride it, but then I heard Dad's voice. *Don't ride the rides at a carnival. They haul them in. they're not as safe as Kennywood.* No ride today.

I ran into my cousin Jim. We walked the midway and meandered through the exhibit hall once more. A free pencil and ruler from an insurance guy was easy to carry in our pockets.

"Did you play any games?" Jim asked me.

"Not yet."

"Do you want to play?"

"Which one," I asked.

"I saw some guy win a bear that was three feet tall," he told me.

He had hooked me. I wanted a bear.

We walked by the duck site. I really wanted a bear. Just then another guy won a bear.

"Grab a duck, win a bear, young man!" The carny called, as he looked right at me.

I handed him 20 cents and picked up a duck.

"You win a drinking glass.

I wanted a bear, so I gave him another 20 cents.

"You win another drinking glass. It's your lucky day! Try your luck again," Carny said. "You wanna try again?"

"One more time!" I told him.

"Look at that, he won another prize. He won a finger trap. Ya wanna try once more?"

"I'm done," I told him. "Let's go, Jim."

We met my dad, just in time to go home.

"Where'd you get the glasses?" he asked.

"I won them when I picked up a duck."

"Why?"

"Wanted to win a stuffed bear. Saw two guys win one."

"Don't you know those guys work for the carnival?"

"Really?"

Uncle Everett was right, but I still had 55 cents.

Post script:
When I went to the fair in 2014, the 4-H milkshake cost $4.00.

26. WASHINGTON COUNTY FAIR, 1954, PART II

On Friday of that same week, I finally got a chance to go the fair at night. Uncle Ross was a fan of work horses. He still had a working team that he used for various farm work. They dragged the plow, pulled the hay wagon and the corn planter. He stopped at our house to let his mother, my grandmother, Gram Myers, visit while he and his wife, Aunt Ethel went to the fair.

"You wanna go to the fair?" Uncle Ross asked me.

"I went yesterday."

"You can see the horse pull tonight" he responded.

"What are they gonna pull?"

"A sled of cement blocks."

"They keep adding weight until only one team can to pull it," Aunt Ethel said.

"Mom, can I go?"

"Will you behave yourself?" Mom asked.

"Of course."

I'm finally going to get to go to the fair at night.

Uncle Ross really got into the competition of the teams. There were two levels, separated by the weight of each group, light weights and heavy weights. I was interested in the beginning, but I didn't care who won or lost. I stayed tuned until near the end of the pulls by the lightweights. When the load got tough for the horses to drag on the dirt covered track, they got low to the ground and nearly crept along as they attempted to be the winner.

"Are the horses going to hurt themselves?" I asked.

"No, they'll stop when the load is too much for them."

"They still look like they're hurting themselves. I'm afraid for them."

When the competition got down to two teams, I asked Aunt Ethel if I could go to the carnival and meet them at the fair entrance at 10 o'clock.

"Are you sure you can be alright by yourself?" she asked.

"I'm sure."

Off I went to the midway and immediately met school friends. I was in good company. We walked through the carnival and were really impressed by the carny's claim that there was a two headed calf inside the tent. We didn't bite.

The next side trip totally changed my feeling about the fair. The new exhibit hall was filled with displays from local businesses, politicians and the Red Cross. I picked up a first aid chart, then I saw something I'd never seen before. *What was the silver tube?* I got closer and noticed that a child's head (a mannequin) could be seen from one end. An older woman in a gray uniform approached me as I passed by. My school friends were scared and disappeared.

"This is an iron lung," she told me. "Do you know what it's for?"

"No. I've never seen one. Do real people get in one?"

"Yes. This machine helps a person to breathe."

"Why can't they breathe?" I probed.

"The muscles that help a polio victim to breathe no longer work."

POLIO!

The joyous attitude at the fair suddenly turned to one of fear. Kids had been warned by their parents to stay away from the streams and ponds from swimming due to the threat of polio, but the iron lung made it very real.

The kind lady knew that she had touched a raw nerve. I could feel the color fading from my face.

I knew that polio was a threat, but the iron lung really brought the seriousness of the disease to the forefront at a place that I had always associated with fun. I walked out of the hall and wandered aimlessly as I pondered the information that I had happened upon. Back I went to the horse pulling contest. Maybe the comfort of family would help to lessen the impact of what I'd just seen.

"You're back already?" Aunt Ethel asked.

"Yeah, I'm ready to go home."

"The horse pull should be done soon."

I didn't remember much about the horses. My mind was on the iron lung. I don't remember the fear wearing on in the next few days. School started and I basically forgot about the iron lung.

So much for going to the fair at night.

Follow up:
During the next school year the Borland Manor Elementary School that I attended was one of the first to receive the Salk Polio Vaccine. I could breathe easier.

27. EIGHTY FOUR'S COOLEST KIDS

The late summer sun beamed a hazy, lazy mood over the farm house on Wilson Road. The white, two-story clapboard house with the red tin roof was home to three generations of Neills: Gram Neill, Mom and Dad, my brother Curt and me. On this hot summer day, the "air conditioning" was in full swing—every window and door in the house was opened for cross-ventilation. When that failed, the fan took over.

Nobody we knew had an air conditioner in their house. We didn't even know a public place that had air conditioning—not our doctor, not the A&P, not even the local hospital. The nearest we had was a small oscillating fan. About all it did was move the hot air around the already hot room.

My grandmother had a cardboard fan that telescoped into a small package that could slip into her pocketbook. She took it to church and used the fan to cool her face. There were also fans made from a piece of cardboard with a flat stick attached for a handle that stayed in the hymnal holders of the church. These fans had beautiful pictures on one side and an advertisement for "Hinton and Griffith Funeral Home, West Pike Street, Canonsburg, Pa., Phone 89," on the other side. It always seemed that women did the fanning. I don't ever remember seeing anyone of the old guys using a fan, and they all wore suits.

Because we lived on a working farm, chores took up most of our time, especially in the summer. Many times as soon as our work was done we would escape to the stream to cool off.

We started in our earliest years by going to the small creek below the barn. Even though the rocks were slippery and watercress grew along the edge, we thought it was the coolest place. At the ages of six and eight, you could hardly call what we were doing swimming. We splashed around, looked for minnows, threw rocks and tried to dunk each other.

One day when I was five and Curt was seven, we thought we'd teach the cat how to swim. We didn't know that cats don't swim very well and really hate water. We carried her down to the creek side; I held her while Curt went to the other side. I thought if I put her in the water she could swim to dry land, and she did. But we were determined to get her to swim some more. Curt retrieved the tired cat and put her back in the water to swim back. This didn't last too long. The cat expired. We felt bad about this and immediately took the stiffening cat to show my mother. I hadn't yet learned the correct term for fatality and told my mother that "we had deaded the cat." We had learned our lesson about cats and never tried to teach another one to swim.

As we got older we liked to plunge into the water of the Little Chartiers Creek. By walking along the stream at the end of our lane it was about a quarter of a mile from home, but a half mile via the road. It was much wider than the small creek that ran near the barn. We claimed a wide spot in the stream that had been created when a railroad built large cement abutments.

On one very hot summer day a bunch of my cousins and neighbors came over to help bale hay. By the end of the day we were so itchy from the hay dust that was sticking to us that my brother Curt said, "Let's go swimming."

A chorus erupted, "Yeah, yeah, let's go."

"Keith, get the inner tube out of the shed."

As farm kids, we didn't have the usual pool toys that kids have today. We had old inner tubes that were discards from car and tractor tires. We had access to the inner tube patch kits—some red and some black. We thought they were pretty snazzy. An inner tube might have as many as 20 patches. A leak shows up very fast when it hits the water. *Sssss*. Back to the patch shop. My dad had to know that the patches were disappearing rather quickly in the summer. A tractor inner tube was great because the opening in the center was so large. We could easily float around and play dunking games.

One of the problems with a tractor tire tube is the large stem through which the tube is filled with air. It is about twice the size of an automobile inner tube stem. We had to be very careful when hopping into the center of the tube. The valve tip can be disastrous to ribs, backs and any skin spot that gets scraped. My cousin taped one of the valve tips down with massive amounts of tape. It worked well to prevent scratches but was quite a deterrent to fixing a hissing inner tube.

When anybody dove into the water they came up with strings of algae hanging on shoulders and sticking to arms. Mud squished between toes and left a muddy scum on the arch as it dried. Although we cooled off, we had to take a bath when we got home because we were dirtier than we had been when we jumped into the old swimming hole. We were the coolest kids along Wilson Road. Really, we were the only kids on Wilson Road.

28. THE COLOR BARRIER

There seemed to be a clash between our family and some of our neighbors. It had to do with colors. Ours was orange and theirs was green. We are of Irish heritage, but our orange had nothing to do with the colors of the Irish flag. After all both orange and green are sections of that flag.

And although the neighbor who came from Ireland didn't have a problem with orange or green, he preferred red. The farm neighbors who had a "liking" for green were Polish. And then there's Benny Levin who liked gray. It all had to do with the brand name of tractor the farmer used. And were they loyal? Maybe.

Several times during the year these various colored tractors came together. They joined forces with their neighbors who all worked together to complete each other's yearly threshing and the filling of silos. And in spite of the differences of color, everyone got along.

The threshing machine was used to separate grain from the straw. It was stationary. The grains that were threshed were barley, wheat and oats. After the separation the straw was baled and the grain was put into sacks. These products were then stored in the barn. Threshing was a huge job and the many farmers who came to the site made it possible to complete the task in one day. The 1922 diary from my great-grandmother reports what happened one day, "Still thrashing. Thrashed 745 bushel of wheat, 250 bushel of oats and baled 35 tons of straw."

The farmer where the threshing was taking place paid the man who owned the threshing machine a fixed rate per day. That's why all the neighboring farmers worked together to get the job completed in one day. I only remember threshing happening one time at our farm. Then we got a combine. The combine did just that. It combined the process of cutting and separating the grain from the straw and chaff.

Silo filling was also a cooperative effort. The farmers hauled the green hay or the corn, ears and stalks to a machine called a blower. This blower was propelled by a belt driven motor on the tractor. That forced the chopped product up the sixty-foot pipe to where it fell in the 20-foot diameter silo. This product "cured" in the silo and was stored there until it was fed to the cows during the winter.

At lunch time the farm women prepared a huge meal for the workers. There is still an expression among farm women when there is a very large meal. "Do you think you're cooking for thrashers?" Ten or so good cooks prepared foods fit for the kings, their farmer husbands.

Another entry from my great-grandmother's 1922 diary is as follows, "They commenced to thrash wheat in the morning. Thrashed all day. Had 18 men at dinner and 17 for supper."

This is where you heard the guys teasing each other about the tractor that they drove to the work site that day. It was supposed to be good natured, but some guys were very serious. Today it reminds me of the guys talking about sports teams or which race car driver is the best. I still see pick-up trucks with disparaging signs concerning other brands of trucks.

Although my family farm was orange, I liked the green. Why did I like the green? Because when we went to the county fair, the "John Deere" display of tractors was the largest and had the most advantageous display spot as you entered the fair grounds. Can you imagine the "disgrace" of the father, the orange man to find his son sitting atop a green John Deere tractor? The other draw to this "green" tractor display was that they had toys that represented each of the farm implements and tractors that they sold. They even had a small tractor that resembled a tricycle. I asked for one of the toys. I knew it would be too much to ask for the pedal tractor. Orange didn't have anything like these toys at that time.

"Dad, can I get one of these toy tractors?"

"No, you have more toys at home than you can play with."

"I know, but I don't have a toy tractor."

"And you're not going to have one now."

When dad won't get you what you want, then you try to get it by dealing with mom. She had more bargaining power with him than I did.

"Mom, can I get that tractor? Will you get it for me?"

"Ask your dad."

"I already asked him."

"If your dad said you can't get it, you can't get it. Didn't he already give you two dollars to spend today?"

"Yes!"

"Then you've already gotten your share today. Don't upset him by pestering him."

It wasn't the ending that I wanted from our trips to the county fair. Although I had learned a little bit about budgeting, after all, I had gotten two dollars for the day. I remember casing the food booths to find the best deal and surveying the games and rides to see if any were worth the money. I hadn't thought of saving enough money to buy the toy, although two dollars wasn't enough to buy it.

Once the harvest was over, we began getting ready for the holidays. I liked to go shopping with my mother in Washington, Pennsylvania. After lunch at the G.C. Murphy counter we headed to her favorite store—J.C. Penney. My Mom was looking at bedding when I spotted Santa Claus.

"Hey, Mom! Look who's sitting over there."

"Are you ready to talk to him?"

"I don't think I want to talk to him. I'm afraid of him."

With a little cajoling, she convinced me to have an audience. I did.

Santa Claus asked about my behavior. I probably lied. Then he asked me what I wanted him to bring. I couldn't think, so I looked at my mother.

"Tell him what you want."

"What do I want?"

"What did you see at the fair?"

"Oh, I want a toy John Deere tractor."

The dialogue continued with the man in red, and when it was over I forgot about the request.

"Is anybody coming to see what Santa Claus left under the tree?"

It's hard to believe that my brother and I had slept in. After all it was Christmas morning.

"I don't believe it. Look what's under the Christmas tree. It's the John Deere tractor. How did Santa Claus know that's what I wanted? And there's a combine too."

Our family had finally broken the color barrier. Actually my dad never really cared about the model or color of the tractor anyone drove. He always said that he drove the one that started every time and could haul the equipment that he owned. I had learned a valuable lesson about my dad's position on life's issues.

29. MY DAD, THE FARMER

My dad, Frank Neill, gave new meaning to the term gentleman farmer. He was a working gentleman farmer. His daily uniform was a green long-sleeved shirt and pants. But when Dad went to church or some social function, you would not have known he was a farmer. He dressed smartly and I never saw him without a fedora when he went out. Because dad had flat feet, the only shoe that he could put his arch support in was a black high-topped dress shoe, like policemen wore. Once his pant leg covered the top of the boot, they looked like dress shoes.

When he was 29, his father died suddenly. Being the eldest son of the family, the operation of the farm fell on his shoulders, although my Grandmother micro-managed the entire operation. Because it was a dairy farm, this responsibility became like a prison without bars. The cows never took a vacation and neither did my dad. Every morning and every evening the cows needed to be milked.

The time between milking was loaded with other farm chores. City folks think there's nothing to do in the winter time. But in the winter the cows stayed in the barn the majority of the day. This meant the cows were left out for a short time. The manure and old bedding were removed, fresh bedding was spread, the feed trough was filled with fresh feed and the cows came back into the barn.

In addition to these chores, the milk tank where the raw milk was stored had to washed and disinfected after the milk truck came and hauled it away. This was all back breaking work. In later years my Dad wore a back brace to help alleviate the back pain. Dad spent hours repairing hay wagons, mowing machines and hay balers as well as overhauling tractors. He could fix just about anything, and he did. If he didn't have the needed tools, he knew somebody who did.

Spring and summer were the busiest times on the farm. He spread manure, plowed and planted seeds and maintained fences and farm buildings. Once the crops were mature, he baled hay, cut grain and cultivated the corn. All this happened along with the milking which never ended.

The fall brought on the corn crop and if the season was dry he would plow for the spring planting.

Farming is a solitary job. Dad missed the interaction with other people. He looked forward to going to the Eighty Four Auction on Mondays even if he didn't have extra eggs, baby calves or old baloney cows to sell. This gave him a chance to talk to other farmers and find out what was going on in the farm community. Often on Saturday nights the whole family went to Canonsburg. While Mom, Curt and I shopped, Dad met up with his friends and shot pool in the room over Dr. Wilson's office along Pike Street.

As a young child, I could be a thorn in my dad's side. Attention-getting behavior was part of my method, especially when visitors came to the house or when I met them in a social situation. Dad would quietly remind me of the consequences of unacceptable behavior. But I often tested the waters of what I could get away with. I don't ever remember him yelling or getting into a verbal battle, but I knew when he gave me the evil eye that I'd better straighten up. I never thought he'd discipline me in front of visitors. I remember when we invited our new neighbors to go to church. I wanted to sit beside them and I did. When my behavior didn't meet Dad's standard, he reached across the others and hauled me off to the car, where he gave me a swat on the behind.

"I'm going to tell Mom what you did to me." No response.

Once I'd settled down, we returned to our seats, where I sat lightly, next to him.

I remember the time we attended a relative's fiftieth wedding anniversary celebration. I was probably five and don't remember what I did, but I didn't do what was expected. Dad wrapped his thumb and index finger around my wrist and held me next to him for what seemed like an hour. Asking Mom for help didn't work. And wailing, "You're hurting me," didn't help. He let go of my arm when I promised I'd march to his music. I would often forget the promise I made.

In moments like this, his favorite expression was, "Somebody's going to furnish the ass for an ass kicking." I never got kicked.

Because my mother didn't drive, one of my earliest memories of my dad was the trips we took together to the eye therapist. We drove to the Jenkins Arcade every Thursday for two years. It was a good time to talk and learn about his whims and peculiarities. I remember vividly watching a crane with a swinging ball that was knocking down some of the older buildings—the Pittsburgh Renaissance.

Sometimes we drove along Saw Mill Run Boulevard. A new restaurant was under construction. It was named Eat'n Park.

I said, "Dad, let's stop and get a Big Boy." That was the name of the sandwich on the advertisement.

"We don't have time to stop. We have food at home."

I made up for the lost Eat'n Park time while in high school. It was a hangout for some of my best friends. The car hops took our order and delivered our food. A tray hung over the open window.

As I got older, he and I would have conversations as we worked on projects. He told me once as we walked along the creek that we'd never see that water again. He was a deep thinker who constantly read in his free time. His money advice was, "Watch your nickels and the dollars will take care of themselves." He was a great example of how to live a productive and worthwhile life. The best piece of advice Dad ever gave was not to become a farmer. He didn't always agree with my decisions, but allowed me to stumble sometimes. He was also supportive and told me that he was glad that I'd become a high school teacher.

Dad and I often had philosophical talks. As he lay dying at Mercy Hospital in Pittsburgh after six or seven heart attacks, he told me not to be concerned about this stage of his life. "It's only the last step." He died that evening near midnight on July 4th, 1986. The next day I thought, wow he ministered to me as he lay dying.

30. MAKING DEPOSITS

My Dad and brother got tired of the Rhode Island Reds coming to the back porch and leaving a deposit. The main cash crop of the Western Pennsylvania farm was the Holsteins. They were the big black and white cows that roamed the green pastures in the summer and ate the hay and other harvested crops in the winter. The cows were my Dad's money makers. They produced milk. This paid the bills.

The chickens on the other hand were my Mother's cash crop, and they did leave more than just the deposits on the sidewalk. Every spring 100 baby chicks arrived in a cardboard box. The box, with holes in the top to allow the baby chicks to breathe, provided a chorus of chirpers, each trying to out-chirp the other.

"We're here. Do you see us? Get us out of this box," they cheeped.

The chicks got out of the box and went from cute and furry to clucking and crowing animals within five months. The roosters ended up on dinner tables, ours and others', while the hens became shareholders in the farm. Maybe they were the tenant farmers. It didn't take much mash for the pullets because they were great at free ranging the property to support their lifestyle. They had their own operation of scavenging the open fields and manure piles where they were able to extract that special tidbit the others might have missed. It was their way of finding bugs and seeds. They always seemed to know where the bugs and worms could be found.

Our baby Holstein calves, on the other hand, arrived in the spring when the pregnant cows started dropping their calves on the fresh green grass of the meadow. It would be two years before they became part of the farm production.

The Rhode Island Reds were a proud group of fowl, who guarded the yard, the chicken coop and the expanse of ground that stretched endlessly toward the barn—the cow's domain. The chickens had an advantage; they could fly. They could get over the board fence and scratch the pigs' deposits or, they could go under the electric fence and attempt to steal the Holstein deposits. But every one of the Rhode Island Reds also left deposits. They left eggs. Somehow, despite their constant travel along the roads and paths of the farm, they always made it back to the coop to deposit their eggs. We collected the eggs every evening and took them to the back porch where they were cleaned and placed in wicker baskets to be stored in the cellar. They soon became the exchange product for quick cash. Once the chickens flew the coop, they had the run of the place.

The Holsteins, however were at the mercy of the farmer. We had to open the gate for them to get around the farm.

Each week my dad took corn, oats, wheat and barley to the Canonsburg Feed Mill where these raw materials were ground into cow feed. A small portion was ground into chicken feed (mash), a more finely ground product with differing portions of the grains. Although the feed came from the farm cache, the money earned from the eggs was at my Mother's discretion.

The bulk of our milk left the farm in metal cans that the milkman picked up every morning and took to a processing plant. Local buyers could fill their own containers with raw milk from the remaining large cans in the milk cooler and deposit 50 cents per gallon in the old coffee can in the milk house. When the milk price increased by ten cents, Mr. Pollock asked if he could still pay 50 cents. He was retired and on a fixed income. He continued to pay 50 cents.

Egg buyers had to come when my mother was available. Eggs sold for 50 cents per dozen. That money went straight to the smooth aluminum cup that lived on the top shelf of the Hoosier Cabinet. We had regular patrons who became like family as well as family members who bought on a regular basis. It was all part of the country social interaction.

The egg money took care of incidentals that arose unexpectedly. It never seemed to run dry. I remember "going to the cup" to get money to pay the bread man and the ice cream man or to pay Aunt Grace for freshly churned butter. If I needed lunch money, Mom would tell me, "Get 25 cents from the egg money."

Probably the most memorable use of the egg money came when I left for college. I had sent a $15 check to California State College for the application fee. It became my security deposit when I decided to go there. On the day of registration, my mother and I counted $85 out of the egg money to pay the other portion of the fall 1961 semester's tuition. The second semester, I carried $100 in cash—more egg money. The treasurer told me it was the last time cash would be accepted for tuition payment.

The next year, the tuition went up by $25. We had to sell more eggs. And that year, a different kind of deposit was made—into a checking account.

31. AN UNHAPPY DAY ON THE FARM

It was a chilly December day. I knew it was coming. I sat on the porch with my hands over my ears. Then I heard it.

BANG! The gunshot echoed. I tried to hold back my tears.

Piggy fell over with a thud as the 22-caliber bullet pierced its skull, right between the eyes. I had learned to stay away from the pig pen when this happened. I had seen it once and I said, "Never again." I couldn't stand to see one of my sty friends dying. It's not that most of my friends were pigs; it's just that when you see and talk to them every day they become like family.

I knew that he lay there bleeding on the straw where he had been stuck in the jugular vein with a butchering knife. That was the follow up to the killing. It would be a few minutes, long minutes until he would be pulled from the pig sty and taken to the back of the barn.

Here the animal was submerged into an old clawfoot bath tub that was filled with boiling water. The hot water acted like shaving cream as it loosened the hair. After a few minutes, Piggy was hauled from the hot water using ropes, and placed on a makeshift table that had sawhorse legs. The bell scraper was the handy gadget for scraping the water soaked hair.

After Piggy had been scraped hairless, I didn't recognize him anymore. Then I could look at the carcass, because it no longer represented my pet pig. After he was hairless, my father proceeded to remove the internal organs and started dismembering him.

Because we didn't have a large enough cooler, the remains were hoisted to the second level of the tractor shed for cooling and safe storage. We always had to slaughter animals in the cold months to permit proper cooling.

I never had to take part in the cutting and processing of the dead beast. This always happened when I was in school. I'm glad I never learned how to do this.

One of my daily chores was to feed the slop, a mixture of ground grain and water, to the pigs. Piggy came to greet me every day when I delivered breakfast or dinner. Now he was gone. Some of the old sty friends were still there, but they'd be going to the animal auction or to the same fate that Piggy had met.

My father never developed a bond with the farm animals. He knew of their final intention. He must have read my thoughts and ideas because he told me that I should never become a farmer.

Farm kids must learn early on that they should not make pets of animals that are raised for profit. This includes kids who raise animals to show at the fair. Although the show animal brings lots of cash, it's not uncommon to see sobbing youngsters saying good-bye to their prize winner. Piggy never got a prize, but I know the feeling. But, young kids don't always get the memo.

32. THE MINGO SPRING HOUSE

I don't know why my Gram insisted on using the spring house as the extra refrigerator. Nineteen forty-eight was a big year at the Myers family house near Mingo Creek – they got electricity. But in the early 1950s she still liked to keep certain items in the cold water of the little log building just over the hill from the house. She always had plenty of room in the fridge, but insisted on still using the Spring House for the overflow. Maybe she didn't trust that newfangled electricity that ran the fridge.

"Why do you keep the butter and milk in the spring house?" I asked Gram.

"The butter doesn't get as hard in the spring house."

"How about the milk?"

"I just like it better in the spring house," she answered.

I wasn't about to change her mind. Old habits are hard to break.

The spring that fed the water into this building seeped out of the hillside and was housed in a separate whitewashed shed to protect the purity of the water and to keep unwanted animals from drinking and bathing in the icy cold of the water. In spite of this protection, crayfish and minnows lived there. From this building, it flowed underground through a small stream that had been harnessed in terra cotta pipes and fed into a second two-story log building. The first floor of this building contained a trough the size of a single bed that held milk cans, and a protected chamber to hold the kitchen overflow. The water temperature of springs usually ranges between 56 and 59 degrees, Fahrenheit.

After the spring water flowed through the cooling chamber of the spring house, it ran from the building and formed a small stream that eventually flowed into Mingo Creek (named for the Indian Tribe), nearly a half mile from its source.

One of my chores, as a young kid, was to be the runner from the kitchen to the outside cold storage. It was like running from home plate to first base and back. Gram used to say, "You run and get the lemonade. Your legs are younger than mine." I liked to see how fast I could make the round trip without dropping any precious cargo.

My Gram Myers and Uncle Ross were the milk crew every morning and evening. They strained the freshly produced milk through a cotton filter into five-gallon milk cans in the barn. Then Uncle Ross hauled the cans in a hand cart to the spring house. It was a football field's length away from the barn, down a steep grade. The cans were submerged into the cold spring water until they were taken to the Meadow Gold milk receiving center in Pittsburgh. Uncle Ross hauled these milk cans in addition to those of many farmers in the surrounding area. Everybody knew him as the milk truck driver.

I was six when I was sent to my Gram's house to stay out of trouble as I healed from a gash on my left foot. Dr. Wilson had stitched it in his office in Canonsburg and ordered me to rest and keep my foot elevated as much as possible. The second day at my Gram's I went out to explore the barn. On the way back to the house, I got off the path and ended up in the mud of the watering trough overflow.

"Doris, help me," I yelled to my old 14-year-old cousin.

"What did you do?"

"I got my foot dirty."

"Why did you do that?" she asked.

"I don't know."

I could tell by her tone that she wasn't happy about my trek into the mud.

The spring house became the first aid center. Doris made me hop on my good foot to the edge of the ice cold water, farther than first base, where she washed the mud soaked gauze from my foot. She was not happy and was less than gentle as she cleansed the partially healed foot.

"You know this could get infected and you could lose your foot," she angrily snarled. "I told you to keep that foot clean."

"Ouch!" I yelled. "That water is cold. It hurts my foot."

"Be quiet!" She snapped. "You didn't listen to Gram." I cooled it.

I hopped back to the house, uphill this time, where Doris re-wrapped my foot and threatened to lock me in the house. She really couldn't lock me in. They didn't have a key to the house. I survived, but still have the scar.

The spring house is still on the property, now owned by Washington County. The entire family farm is now part of Mingo County Park. Although the spring house is now in deteriorating condition, it is preserved forever in the historical book listed on the following page.

Several interesting early buildings have been saved within the boundaries of Mingo Creek County Park. This log springhouse with an overhanging loft is one of them. It is reasonably well preserved, although outside steps which led to the loft door (not visible) are missing. Buildings like this were common in the late 1700s and early 1800s, but few have survived. This springhouse contained a trough which provided drinking water and kept milk, butter and other perishables cool in hot weather.

Picture and explanation from *Preserving Our Past – Landmark Architecture of Washington County, Pennsylvania,* Washington County History and Landmarks Foundation In cooperation with the Bicentennial Commission of Pennsylvania, 1975.

33. WISH BOOK WORLD

Somehow the Sears Christmas catalog arrived at our house in late October, almost two months before Christmas. That's really unfair to an eight-year-old. Did I have to give up comic books and listening to the "Hopalong Cassidy" or "Big John and Sparky" shows on the radio? Well, in reality, I could look at the catalog and listen to the radio. It was like we had won the lottery. Was I multi-tasking?

The nearly two-inch-thick general catalog came once a year, but only had a small section for toys. This unabridged Christmas version caused my brain to dream, much like my mouth watered when I smelled oatmeal raisin cookies baking in our kitchen.

"The wish book came today," Mom said as we came in the door from school.

That meant that I'd spend precious study time searching for the exceptional toy that I'd place on my wish list. With weeks to go before Christmas, I might even rank order the desired items. I knew the Santa Claus who came to our house would never bring everything my heart desired.

I didn't always do this activity alone. I can remember scheming with my brother Curt and planning to see who could request which toy and maybe arrange to have Santa Claus bring the most loot between us with the least amount of overlapping of the same items.

You could place an order at the catalog center at the store or complete the order form that came in the back of the tome. The Santa of our house ordered at the store. Payment was made to the store, and the package was delivered to our house. I remember when the badminton set came in the mail. It wasn't supposed to arrive on a Saturday; but it did and was quickly whisked away from curious eyes. Santa delivered it on Christmas morning.

When we were older, it seemed that we always got clothes, usually a flannel shirt and new jeans. But this was also the time when we started getting board games. One year we got Monopoly and a chest of games that included chess, checkers, Chinese checkers and a series of other games. Of course we lost the marbles for the set and usually played checkers with the set that we already had. (There's a joke there somewhere about losing one's marbles.)

One of the favorite gifts that we got as young children was the farm set. It included all the implements that were found on a farm at that time, even the work horses, which we had until about 1950. Our horses were named Fan and Prince.

Maybe Santa Dad was trying to plant the idea that one of us would become a farmer and take over the family farm. Neither of us became a farmer. I wish I still had the farm set.

By the time I was in eighth grade, I wanted a transistor radio.

When transistor radios were first introduced in 1954, they cost $49.95 (equivalent to $439.00 in 2016). Santa letters were gone by this time. When I was in eighth grade the dinner discussion in December seemed to center around Christmas. I'm sure I let it be known that I wanted a transistor radio and Mom and Dad were trying to get an idea of what they should get for us.

I got mine in 1957. I was not allowed to take it to school or listen to it when I went to bed. I had taken it to bed early on and caused the nine volt battery to die when I fell asleep.

Mr. John Knupp had worked on our farm as a hired hand and he often came back in old age because he liked the work, the interaction and the good meals that my mother prepared every day at noon. The year after I got the radio, John was at our farm helping to "husk" some animal corn from corn shocks. I had taken my radio along.

My dad wasn't too happy about this because he thought that I couldn't help remove the corn husk because the radio would be a distraction. Mr. Knupp said, "I think I've seen it all now. He's listening to the radio in the corn field!"

I can just imagine what Mr. Knupp would think if he were alive today with all the media that is available and portable.

My radio was the one gift from my youth that I used for many years. I listened to it when I worked on boring jobs and while driving Dad's '52 Chevy, which didn't have a radio.

I don't listen to the radio as much today as in those teen years. Today, I'm happy with a book and quiet time.

34. THE KNICKERBOCKER CLUB

My brother was really lucky. He was too tall and his waist was too small to fit the new suit without major alterations. My mother would never spend the money doing that; after all, the new hand-me-down clothes were free and she wanted to keep them that way.

I was not against wearing hand-me-down clothes. When you're the second child in the family and the same sex as the first, that's what happens. Among the cousins, I was third in birth order. Those lucky first-born kids got all the new clothes. The fourth, fifth and sixth-born male cousins were very lucky. I did a pretty good job of wearing out the hand-me-downs. I don't remember whether they appreciated my saving them from clothes that didn't fit well and had patches all over them.

We didn't have many relatives who lived in the city, but we had many friends who kept us in a supply of used clothing. My mother and grandmother felt it was a sin if we didn't use these donated clothes. I had no say in what came to our house as "gifts." I don't think Goodwill was around yet.

I did like some hand-me-downs. It was a happy day when I got a great striped play suit in a new bag of used clothes. This one I wore every day in the summer–when it was clean. I even remember taking it off the clothesline when it was partially dry because it was a favorite. It was a sad day the next summer when I put it on and it didn't fit.

My mother rummaged through the newly acquired bags of clothes that had been left at our house the night before when our Pittsburgh connection came to visit. I wish I had seen some of the clothes first; I'd have tried to hide them. I don't really know where I would have hidden them. Our house was large, but there weren't enough hiding places that she wouldn't have found them.

"I hate this suit. Do I have to wear it?"

My mother told me how nice it was and how I should appreciate it and the kindness of the Pittsburgh friends who thought of me.

"Yes, you have to wear it. Look at the label. It was bought at Joseph

Horne."

"Who is Joseph Horne? Did the Pittsburgh friends go to school with him? That's not their name."

"Joseph Horne is not a person. Well, he was, but now that's the name of a department store that his family started. The store is known for fine clothes and other things."

"I wish Curt could wear it or they'd have given it to some other *lucky* boy."

"Just put the entire suit on with your white dress shirt. You'll see how nice it looks."

"I know I'm not going to like it," I told her.

"Look." Mom said, "There's even a necktie to match. Your friends will be jealous."

"Jealous of hand-me-downs that don't fit right?" They'll know that we'd never buy anything like this."

"If you don't tell them, no one will know."

"I don't think so. Nobody I know has ever worn anything like this."

So the discussion of the new-to-me suit continued. I tried the suit on and the sad part was that it fit. I really didn't look as bad as I thought I would.

"Mom, what are these funny things on the bottom of the pant legs?"

"I don't know. Let me see?"

"Oh, these pants are called knickers. They are made that way so you can wear socks to meet the bottom of the pants. Let's look in the pocket to see if we can find any socks. Oh yes, here are socks that match the suit and necktie. Boy are you lucky! Try them on too."

"Do I have to? Nobody wears clothes like these. They look like they're worn out already."

"Just try them on, please."

So the knickers and the socks came together. The suit wasn't too bad, but the knickers—HELP!

"This outfit is out of the ark."

I think I wore the suit a couple of times to church, but I usually opted for the clothes that I liked. Thank goodness I didn't have to wear it to school. This outfit was considered "Sunday clothes." I was nine or ten when this all happened. It was at the age where peer pressure becomes more important than what your mother thinks.

Unlike the striped play suit, I tried to forget about this item of clothing. I did pretty well. I don't remember how long I had this suit, but I was glad when it got passed on to someone else.

Jump ahead about 30 years. Our family was on vacation at the seashore. We decided to check out the Army Navy surplus store that we had walked past several times. What do you think my son was attracted to? Wool knickers.

"Dad, these are so cool. I'm going to get them."

"Are you sure you will wear them when you get home? You know you need socks to match them."

"I know. I already know the pair that I'll wear with them. Can I get them?"

"If that's what you want to spend your money on, it's fine with me. Just make sure that you will wear them when you get home."

And wear them he did. We were invited back to an anniversary at the church where I grew up and there he is, pictured with the knickers and socks that match. I saw his knickers several times after that and then he was off to college. I'm sure they were a hit there, unlike the hand-me-downs that I had hated. But his weren't hand-me-downs.

I asked him recently about his knickers.

"Dad that was about thirty pounds ago."

Like father, like son.

His were unique and drew attention. Mine drew attention that I didn't need.

35. MISS TRINITY

People who didn't grow up in Washington County, Pennsylvania sometimes think that Trinity High School must be a church related school. After all, where else do you hear of the Trinity, but in church? But this was not the case with Trinity High School, located just outside the city of Washington. It had been a private military school started in 1879 and was frequently visited by Ulysses S. Grant. It became a public school in 1925. My aunt, my uncle, my cousin and my brother attended this high school. It is still easily recognized by the bell tower that remains atop the original building.

Every year the Trinity High School Chapter, Future Farmers of America (FFA) in Washington, Pennsylvania celebrates the end of school with a banquet in the early spring. Since three of the family had taken the agriculture course at the high school, they were always invited back to the banquet that the FFA put on each year. My dad had gone to Canonsburg High School, so he was not a member, but he always got invited or was the guest of my Uncle Judson Neill, who had won the state award as the FFA, Pennsylvania farmer of the year in 1940. That was the year he graduated from Trinity.

It's a typical farm banquet, that is, it's late in the day. Why? Because many dairy farmers had to milk the cows before they came to the banquet. Sometimes it was held at the high school and other times it was held at a restaurant in the area. Like a reunion, it was a good time for attendees to catch up with old friends, develop new relationships and listen to speakers talk about the latest trends in farming and agricultural education.

One year, in either 1950 or 1951, my dad went to the celebration and won a door prize. There were many prizes that year, and he won one of the best ones. He won Miss Trinity. **

When dad came home, he told my mother that he had won the top door prize at the banquet. She didn't believe him. She thought he probably won some farm tool or a pair of work gloves. These are the usual prizes that were awarded at these functions.

"Miss Trinity is coming to live at our house," he told her again.

"You couldn't have won Miss Trinity. She's not to be awarded as a prize," she told him.

"I have to pick her up tomorrow," he told my mom.

We were in awe. What kind of game was my dad playing? We couldn't wait.

"She, Miss Trinity, won't be ready for me to pick her up until one o'clock. I have to wait until she has eaten lunch."

"Where do you have to pick her up?"

"She's out at the farm located just past the high school. I won't be long."

After noon the next day, dad drove away in the small red International pick-up truck that he and my uncle shared. We wondered why he would be going to get Miss Trinity in the pick-up truck. But he did.

It was nearly two hours until he returned home. We were so anxious. We heard him driving up the lane. Mom and I rushed out the back door to see our new guest.

In the back of the truck was a small wooden crate. Inside the crate was a small black piglet with a white belt curving around her back.

"What's he doing with a pig?"

"Here she is. Here's Miss Trinity."

"Where? I don't see her."

"Right here," as he pointed to the pig in the back of the truck.

"I thought Miss Trinity was a person," I said.

"Never told you she was a person," my dad said.

"What are you going to do with her?" my mom asked.

"She's going to live here and grow and have lots of baby pigs. She's going to have the run of the pig lot."

My dad backed the truck up to the pig pen and opened the crate. Miss Trinity stayed to the front of the crate so he had to reach in to get her. When she was placed on the ground, she took off and ran to where the older pigs were.

Miss Trinity certainly was not what we expected, but we grew to love her. In the years to follow, she gave birth to many little piglets. Miss Trinity reigned over the pig lot for six or seven years.

** When I heard this, I thought we were talking about the May Queen (I was young). She was a very important figure at this high school. Trinity High School always had a beautiful May Day celebration on the campus at the school, where they paraded the grounds and circled the May pole and crowned the May Queen.

36. HEIGH, HO SILVER

Silver, the ink black Angus-Holstein, had been on the farm for about a year. Just like all the yearlings, he got moved to the field beside the pig sty. But unlike the other yearlings, Silver was special. He was the only yearling that we named. He got his name because of the silver diamond shape on his forehead.

This yearling field was also used by the pigs and the chickens. They spent the summer together. The cattle ate the grass. The pigs had a chance to soak in the mud puddles and root the sod. The chickens liked some of the same morsels as the pigs, but nobody ever seemed to be possessive of the real estate. There was enough space that the chickens and the pigs searching the same ground didn't battle over who had the territorial rights. It was there that they found the vitamins and minerals they needed. They could also eat small insects, grubs and worms.

My brother Curt and I had the job of hauling buckets of feed to the various animals each day. The pigs got their ground feed inside the pig sty, a place where the cattle couldn't go. The chickens flew back to the hen house where they enjoyed a meal of mash and oyster shell, which produced hard shelled eggs.

When Curt and I carried the feed to the cattle, they rushed toward us, nearly knocking us over to get to the feeder—all the cattle, except one. Silver seemed to want human attention. He stayed close to us, but wasn't pushy. He never got aggressive, but nuzzled his head to our extended hand. It got to the point that when he saw us in the yard, he came to the fence and mooed a soft, "Come by and pet me."

The next thing we knew, he was following us around. We decided that we were going to treat him like a horse, but instead of a bridle, we put a rope around his neck. That way we could lead him around.

He allowed us to brush his coat with the curry comb to rid him of matted hair and teasel. After a short time, one of us could sit on his back and the other could lead him around the feed lot. Silver seemed to enjoy the sport and cooperated with the new form of entertainment. We were thrilled to interact with him. We had never been so close to one of the farm animals. He was our best friend and he made the summer of '53 special. I was ten years old.

By the end of summer, we were able to ride him outside of the lot. We could be on his back and lead him around the farm paths.

Heigh-ho Silver!

Once school began, we could only ride Silver on weekends. We had farm chores and homework to do during the week.

One September day when we got off the school bus, Curt and I zoomed to Silver's field to say hi to him.

"He's not here."

"Maybe he broke the fence." Just then we heard the whistle of the B&O train.

"Surely he didn't go out on the train tracks."

We ran down to the tracks, but he was nowhere in sight.

"Maybe Mom knows where he is. We didn't ask her."

We traced our steps back toward the house and checked the fence again. There was not a break in the fence, anywhere.

"Mom, have you seen Silver?"

"No, I haven't seen him." She answered with a puzzled look on her face.

"We can't find him anywhere."

"I did hear your dad talking about taking the yearling steers to the sale."

37. SOLOMON

When Solomon heard the squeak of the opening tail gate, he knew it was time to jump into the back of the faded red 1955 Chevrolet pick-up truck we affectionately called "Big Red." He liked to ride and stretch his head around the cab to let the wind blow against his hair. He always had a big twist and shake when he reached the destination, so he could get his honey-colored fur back in place.

Sol was the Shepherd Collie mix who came to live at our house when someone wanted rid of him after he grew out of the cute puppy stage. He didn't know that he was a dog, except he wasn't permitted to come into the house. He was a farm dog, and he lived by "farm dog rules." He never protested.

It seemed that Sol could read my Dad's in-head GPS and knew that the jaunt in "Big Red" was to Uncle Judd's farm. It was only a two mile drive, but he was always excited to ride in the truck. He acted like a puppy again. Then there was the reward of visiting with Spot, Uncle's Dalmatian. Although they were both males, they had dog camaraderie. Maybe they thought they were related, almost like in-laws. Their tails wagged, and they danced around and sniffed each other to learn of any new scents that may live at the other's house. They romped and ran around the barnyard until it was time to head for home. When it was time to leave, Dad just opened the tail-gate. The creak of the hinge was like Pavlov alerting him that it was time for another ride.

Sol also knew when it was time to eat. He heard the squeaking of the screen door after supper, and he knew the reward was leftover gravy and Swiss steak, as well as dog food. He and my mother were the best of friends. Mom fed him. She didn't set out to be his best friend, but somehow Sol knew that she had won his heart through his stomach and he rewarded her as a constant companion. When she fed the chickens, gathered eggs or hung clothes on the line, Sol went with her. They had the perfect game of "Follow-the-leader." Sometimes he led, and sometimes she led. There was never a power struggle. The destinations were always the same.

Because he was an outdoor dog, Sol spent the cold winter nights in the warm barn along with thirty "hot-blooded" Holsteins. They never had a disagreement. Sol would even sleep beside one of the cows on the straw covered cement floor. They shared each other's heat.

As time passed, Sol figured out how to get to Uncle's farm without riding in the back of Big Red. We would stop at their farm and Sol would already be there. It had become more difficult for him to jump into the back of the truck, although Dad often helped him into the truck bed. Jumping was difficult, but running was not. He walked to visit Spot. He could still move quickly, and his ears, eyes and nose were easily alerted to sights and to the females of the neighborhood.

Apparently there was a female in the neighborhood of Uncle's farm that vied for the attention of the two farm dogs. Sol and Spot had a fight for the opportunity to have a date with her. As fate would have it, Sol lost. He came home bruised and battered. He never visited Spot's domain again.

It took some time for Sol to nurse his wounds. After this battle he was content to stay at home. He could no longer run with the big dogs. He just stayed on the porch. Although he did recover from the farmyard battle with Spot, his health ultimately went downhill.

As with many Shepherds, Sol's back legs deteriorated and he found it difficult to walk. He would pull with his front feet and drag his rear around the yard. He never ran again, but he never lost his keen ears. And although his nose was damaged, he never lost his ability to detect female dogs. He even tried to jump to attention when he heard the opening of Big Red's tailgate.

Too bad there wasn't a American Association of Retired Dogs (AARD).

Sol is forever at home near the old orchard on the back forty of the farm. He walked there many times when he was young and adventurous. He followed the tractor back and forth while it completed hay baling or corn picking. It was all part of his home, and now he will rest there forever. May he rest in peace.

38. THE TRAIN, THE RAIN AND MY NEW HAT

"Mom, can I go to the school picnic? It's at Kennywood. They're selling tickets at school next week. Can I go? Huh! Can I go?"

"How are you going to get there?" she inquired.

"Remember the last time we went? We rode with Aunt Pearl. Could we go with her again?" I thought I had all the answers on how I could get to Kennywood.

"She didn't think she'd be able to go this year." Mom said.

I hadn't thought about Aunt Pearl not going.

"I can't drive and you know your dad won't take a day away to go to Kennywood. He said the last time he went that he'd never go again."

How could I get to Kennywood?

Then I saw an advertisement in the *Canonsburg Daily Notes* about the train going from Canonsburg to Kennywood. I don't know how I saw the ad as I usually only read the comics.

"Mom, look. There's a train going to Kennywood. I could go on the train."

"Who's going with you?" she asked in her overprotective voice.

"I'll go by myself. I wish Curt hadn't decided to go to help Aunt Grace on that day."

"Well, you're not going by yourself. You may be 12, but you could get in trouble, get lost or somebody could take all your tickets and your money. Anybody else going?"

"Lots of kids from school are going. They're going by themselves."

"Is anybody's mother going with them?"

"I don't think so. Who wants their mother to go with them?" I smart-alecked to her.

I needed to come up with a plan. I'd be the laughing stock of the school if my mother went to Kennywood with me. No plan emerged.

So, mom did go with me. *Oh joy! My mother's going with me, to the school picnic.*

Dad drove us to the train.

In spite of the fact that my mother was with me, I didn't receive much guff. It was my first train ride. I loved it.

We scrambled up the long, steep hill to the park. Steep didn't bother us. Kennywood was at the top.

My mother wasn't in for rides that went in a circle, went fast or had long lines. Roller coasters weren't her thing. She liked the merry-go-round and the bumper cars. So, we rode the bumper cars. It was obvious that neither of us had ever driven. We got bumped all over the floor. At one point, we were even traveling backward. I was able to ride the whip, the rockets and the train with some school pals who were looking for a partner. I walked through Noah's Ark. I couldn't ride through the Old Mill—not with my mother.

Dark clouds appeared after lunch. Boom! Boom! The thunder wagon was rolling and the next thing we knew rain came down in buckets. After a while, it settled to an easy shower. When it rains at Kennywood, the rides stop, except for the Merry-go-round. The other dry escape was the Penny Arcade.

I plunked a lot of pennies in the slots of the arcade games. My prizes were post cards with pictures of Hopalong Cassidy, Roy Rogers and Dale Evans. The cowboy cards sparked interest in the black felt cowboy hats at the Kennywood store. I got one for Curt and one for myself.

Did I say rain? And rain it did. The backs of my legs were covered with brown and black spots from walking on the wet blacktop. We ended up sitting in the restaurant to avoid the coldness of the rain and soaked up the warmth of the restaurant. That was O.K. We didn't have many tickets left for the rides, and it was almost time to board the train. The rain stopped and we headed down the hill to wait on the train. Many damp riders, with kewpie dolls, stuffed animals and attractive hats climbed aboard. But nobody had two black cowboy hats.

The real train ride was actually more exciting than the one at Kennywood. The journey home proved to be entertaining, and it wasn't even part of the amusement park. Jim Rose, from my class, and his friends had squirt guns. Their target was the train's conductor. My mother thought they were walking home. They never sat down, but played Hide and Squirt with the conductor. They constantly walked through the train cars, laying low for him to come by. I wasn't allowed to move from my seat. I would never mistreat the conductor, but I laughed at the slapstick humor. My Mother didn't think it was funny.

Dad picked us up at the train.

The next day, Curt and I were climbing around the old cement railroad abutment that borders our farm.

In earlier days, we often played Cowboys and Indians, but on this day, we were just trekking along the creek and scaling the bank, wearing our new cowboy hats. Then it happened; my hat came off and fell onto the abutment ledge when I was on top of the make-believe mountain. There it was, 10 feet below. Now the game changed. "Let's go home."

"What'll we tell Mom?"

We moped around the house, but never revealed our predicament.

Mom walked through the kitchen with a basket of clean clothes, on her way to the clothesline. "Where's your new hat?" she asked.

"Oh err, ah, I must have left it in the barn. Let's go get it Curt. C'mon."

We zoomed out the door like a bullet, but didn't head for the barn.

"Now what?" I asked Curt.

"We could get the big ladder."

"No, it's too far and too heavy." It was a ten-minute walk.

"Then, what do you think we should do?"

"We have to get it. She'll kill me. She didn't even want to spend that much for hats."

We sulked around some more. Then Curt had an idea. "We could get a long branch and use it to push the hat."

"Let's go." Off to the site of the misfortune. We found several dead branches, but none were long enough to reach the marooned hat. Finally Curt found one that worked perfectly.

"Now we'll get my hat." I told him. "Great idea!"

Curt swished it back and forth, but it didn't quite reach the hat. "Now what?"

We looked around for a longer stick. None was to be found. Then a bright idea flashed my way. "Hey Curt, let's tie some of the grape vine to the branch we have."

We wrapped the grape vine to the stick and it was enough to reach the hat and slide it to safety without falling in the creek.

When we got back, Mom was preparing lunch. "Oh, there's your hat. How'd you get that gray spot on the side?"

I hadn't even noticed. "I guess I rubbed it on the whitewashed post in the barn."

"You better take care of it. It'll be a long time until you get another one."

39. STRAWBERRY FIELDS FOREVER

The Beatles song, "Strawberry Fields Forever," had not been written yet, but if it had, it would have been a great title for our 1957 project. That's the year Gram Neill got the idea to raise strawberries on our farm. Guess who she had in mind to do all the work? None other than Curt and me. This was to be our way to earn money for college.

This was her winter project. If the seed and plant catalogs hadn't arrived, maybe Gram would have stuck to her quilting instead of dreaming up ways for us to make money. She thought 500 plants would be a good place to start. So off went the order.

I sort of forgot about the strawberry plants until Mr. Cooper, our mailman, drove up our quarter-mile, stony driveway and beeped the horn. He never drove his blue 1952 Studebaker up the driveway unless he had a large delivery. Curt and I knew it was an exciting day when the mailman drove up our lane. Hearts were pounding. We ran out to see what he had. Oh no, could it be the strawberry plants?

"Hi, Mr. Cooper. Do you have something big for us?"

"Yeah, wait till I get it."

He got out of his car, opened the trunk and there was a wooden packing crate.

"What is it?"

"Well, I'm not sure, but it came from a nursery."

Curt and I carried the box over on the porch and untwisted the wire.

"Oh no, 500 strawberry plants? That's why Dad plowed and disked that plot next to the pig lot."

We didn't realize how back-breaking the work of planting would be. What was Gram thinking?

Once we got them all planted, the real work began. It was weeding, hoeing and breaking the suckers (the little stems that come out below the crown of the plant that don't produce fruit). Those suckers looked like vines trying to crawl through a hole in the wall. Searching out those old choking weeds was the most difficult, back-breaking part of the whole process. Bending over for long periods of time without stepping on the berry plants became torture. We did this weekly, all summer, knowing we wouldn't get any berries until next summer.

The second year, in addition to keeping weeds out of the strawberry patch, we had to spread straw under them. Picking the berries is a job that requires a keen eye. We couldn't pick a berry if a portion of it was still green. Customers didn't want a berry that looked like a nose with a white tip. They wanted solid red berries.

After we spent all morning picking the berries, we didn't get a break. We had to sell them. We figured the easiest way to do that would be to put a sign at the end of the lane. It didn't attract any strawberry buyers. The berries were coming on fast and we had to figure out a way to sell them. We became door-to-door peddlers. Curt had his driver's license, so we went to people who we knew to ask them if they'd like to buy a quart of strawberries. They didn't always sell, but we were persistent. Curt would drive and I would tote our strawberry carrier that held six baskets of berries. The customer would look over the berries.

"When were they picked? I don't need any today. Could you come back tomorrow?"

We usually sold a few boxes of berries but more often than not, we ended up bringing the remainder home. It's a good thing my Dad loved strawberry shortcake, and my Mom liked to make jam. They weren't wasted. They just didn't put any cash in the till.

The "Strawberry Fields" lasted for three years. By this time we had built up a better group of customers. Some people even called us to ask if we had any berries. But Curt was starting business school and the patch of berries was not producing as well as it had the first two years. We hadn't planned any rotation of the plants by replacing at least a portion of the older plants on a regular basis. Gram Neill had originally financed the purchase of the plants, and I think she saw that we were losing money. We would never have made any money if we'd had to pay for the plants, pay for the gas to hawk the berries, buy the boxes and hire someone to till and prepare the ground.

Our "Strawberry Fields" didn't last "Forever." It was a risk, but it taught me that I'd never want to depend on tilling the ground to make a living.

40. CITY CHICKEN

When my friend Tom told me his family was having city chicken for supper, I thought it was a chicken that had been raised in the city. After all, we had country chicken at our house, but we never called it that. When Tom's mother asked me to eat with them, I said, "Okay."

When I saw the food on the plate, it didn't resemble the chicken that we had at my house. There was a stick poking out from the main meat portion. It didn't look as appetizing as the drumsticks I usually enjoyed. Maybe I'd just eat the potatoes and salad.

I didn't know it yet, but I was soon to learn about city chicken. Mr. B, my ninth grade history teacher, knew that I lived on a farm. Everyone in my class lived in the country, but my family was the only one who tilled the dirt and had a lot of animals scratching that same dirt. There wasn't another dirt farmer amongst my fellow classmates.

Mr. B's son had received a baby chick for Easter; it was pink. Now as any country kid knows, chickens don't come in bright Easter colors. They come in shades of dark red, brown, white and black, but never pink. But, in the 1950s, it was a common practice to go to the G.C. Murphy's or Woolworth's and buy one of these Leghorn baby chicks that had been tinted an Easter color. Sometime later People for the Ethical Treatment of Animals (PETA) would push for laws so these baby animals were not for sale. They were to be applauded for this action. There were horror stories of the treatment of these adorable Easter pets.

Mr. B. wanted to know if my family would be interested in adopting this chick, now a nearly full-grown chicken. Their postage stamp sized yard and one-car garage just wasn't an adequate place to raise this pet. The chicken always wanted to come into their house. I guess he thought he was a member of the family. Besides that, the town had ordinances that prohibited the keeping of farm animals in the city. It was a sad day for this chicken's foster family as they drove to our house with the perky, city-grown Leghorn in a box decked out with towels, a water bowl and a fancy food dish filled with mash. He didn't know it yet, but he was in for a real shock.

We placed him with the other chickens that were about his size. We had gotten one hundred baby chicks earlier in the year. Ours were what the hatchery called standard assortment, which meant that there should be about equal numbers of hens and roosters. We would eat the roosters and the hens would provide us with eggs and a few to sell.

We always called the adopted chicken City Chicken. The back porch seemed to be the place that City Chicken liked best. He would even try to get in the house whenever someone came in or out of the back door. My family got tired pretty quickly of his decorating the cement walkways and porch area that abutted the kitchen door. He never wanted to join with any of the other chickens or play their chicken games. He didn't even become interested in the hens. He was just a different kind of bird.

What were we going to do with him? More than once we had introduced him to the country chickens that appeared to be about his age. He seemed to want no part of their friendly chicken ways. At last we took him to the adult chicken house. By this time they had the freedom to roam on the free range that surrounded their house. But they would always return to the shelter of the house each evening. City Chicken didn't want any part of this. He still wanted to come into the people house.

The adult chicken house had ten nests where the hens could lay eggs. There was also a large area where the adult chickens could roost. That's what chickens like to do when it gets dark and they need to rest. It is their nature to hold onto this frame with their chicken feet. It always looked like work to me. I thought it would be easier to curl up in a corner. But the only time there was curling up was when the hen rested on top of fertile eggs as she waited for them to hatch.

City Chicken was introduced to this coop many times. He just could not adjust to country living. One afternoon my mother came out the kitchen door and found him trying to have sex with one of the overshoes that she wore to tend the animals when the grass was wet. Now I must remind you that I never heard my mother say anything suggestive, but this time I heard her say, "I don't believe it. City Chicken uses a rubber."

It took me a few days to realize that I hadn't seen City Chicken anywhere around the back porch. I asked my mother whether he had been penned in the chicken house with the door hooked. She didn't look at me and didn't respond.

"You killed him didn't you? I don't want to eat him. Tell me what happened to him.

"He went to the auction with some of the old hens."

41. ON TOP OF THE WORLD

Riding atop a wagon full of baled hay was always one of my all-time favorite rides. It didn't compete with Kennywood rides, but was a chance for farm boys to get a rest from the grueling work of the summer—baling hay. It was a dust infested ride behind the hay baler. Hot summer days on the farm make a "buddy" sweat. We didn't perspire, we sweat.

The drying hay laid in the field in neat rows, waiting to be made into bales. This was a hot, dirty job for my dad, my brother and me. Dad drove the tractor that pulled the baler over the hay rows. The baler picked up the loose hay, shaped it into square bales, tied it with twine and expelled it out the chute. It resembled a sausage stuffer.

My job as a twelve-year-old kid was to use a hay hook to pull bales from the baler. Curt grabbed the bales and organized them on the wagon. Our jobs were the dirtiest, because the extra little pieces of hay, dust and hay seeds came out with the newly shaped bales. As the day wore on, all these particles stuck to the sweat of our bodies, even down the back of our shirts. Talk about itch. This gave new meaning to the name "hay seed."

This whole process looked like a lengthy float in the Fourth of July Parade—tractor, baler and hay wagon.

After the hay wagon was full, Curt and I would scramble up to the top to enjoy a brief respite from the dirty work. It was a chance for the sweat to dry up and to take pleasure in the gentle breeze. The tractor, minus the baler, pulled the wagon to the barn. It was even hotter and dustier unloading and stacking the hay bales in the barn than it was out in the field. As we worked, we began to sweat again; it added another layer of dried dust to our body.

How many layers will I have by the end of the day? It's just summer on the farm, and that's what farm kids are expected to do. Let's see, five loads of hay—ten trips back and forth from field to barn—that's many layers of dust-soaked sweat dried to my skin.

In the summer of 1958, the hay season was extended when Dad and Uncle Judd rented the McBride farm, about ten miles from ours. Getting there was easy—drive the side roads until you reach U.S. Route 19. *What?*

We're going to drive farm tractors and other equipment along a U.S. highway?

I never in my wildest dreams thought we'd ever be riding along a national highway, even for one mile, on a tractor. But, the worst was yet to come. We had extra bales of hay at our farm, but had no room to store them. The extras were being stored at the McBride barn. This was the day that I was told I was going to ride atop the load of hay that's traveling ten miles. A ten-minute ride to the barn was one thing, but riding ten miles on top of the hay was not my idea of the summer getaway.

"Why do I have to be the one to do this?"

"Because you're the only one who isn't driving."

"Oh great. I get to be King of the Road, atop the chariot of hay."

So off we went on roads that I had ridden many times, but never on top of a load of baled hay. It was my reign atop the chariot of hay. I looked for neighbors as we left our farm. Not a soul was in their yard. I couldn't wave to any of my friends or their families. It was easy at first and then the route went under some low-hanging wild cherry trees. There was no escaping the scraping of the branches and the dropping of the half-ripe, stone-hard, wild cherries, which pummeled like little cement pebbles.

I tried to get away from the swishing branches and rough leaves that were scraping my body. I laid face down on top of the hay. That didn't help much since the pointy stubble of the cut hay against my face felt like hundreds of needles jabbing my face. Then I started thinking about where we'd run into more low hanging trees. As I traveled the road in my head, I couldn't think of any more trees that would snag me. I was glad that was over.

Then we came to Route 19. Uncle Judd was driving and he had no trouble looking to the left to make the right turn onto the highway. Once we got onto the four lane highway, traffic was able to pass us, like we were standing still. All of a sudden, it wasn't so much fun. Trailer trucks, Greyhound buses and cars sped by and there I was even with the tops of the trailers. It was not fun anymore. I was scared.

I wasn't paying attention when it was time to tell him when to move for a left to turn onto McDowell Road, until I heard from uncle on the tractor

"Blah, Blah. Pay attention!"

I couldn't understand what he was saying, but I knew he wasn't happy.

All of a sudden, I was drawn back to reality. *Oh, I'm supposed to be watching for the chance to move the tractor and wagon to the left.*

I waved my arms in no-no manner and turned my head back and forth yelling in case he could see me.

"Now you can go," I yelled in my loudest voice and motioned with both hands to the left lane, much like a policeman directing traffic at a busy intersection.

Our small parade continued along McDowell Lane as we passed the

Little Lake Theater, Alcoa Dam, and the Mount Lebanon Drive-In Theater. (The drive-in is long gone, but the Little Lake Theater has been putting on shows since 1949.) Drivers were chomping at the bit as they lined up behind us, unable to pass.

We finally got to the barn where the hay would be stored.

Wow! I'm glad that's over. I hope I never have to ride up there again.

And I didn't have to ride up there again. The next time this scenario played out, Dad followed Uncle in his pick-up truck and pulled along the side of the wagon, beeped the horn and motioned to make the left turn. I was very happy. I'd never have to act as "turn indicator" again. It was safer, too.

When school started, my classmate Jack asked me, "Was that you riding on top of a hay wagon this summer? On Route 19?"

"It was, but I've been replaced with a pick-up truck."

Kennywood rides were looking better.

42. PARK THERE

It was a particularly hot June afternoon in the summer of 1949. I was six years old. I had ridden on the fender of the tractor dad was driving out to the hay field. The hay had been cut, raked and baled; it was ready to be put on the wagon and taken to the barn. This was a three-man job; one guy drove the tractor along the rows of baled hay, one guy threw the bales onto the wagon and the third guy stacked them. The problem was, dad was short of help—there was only Dad and our hired man.

As they surveyed the situation, Dad turned to me and said. "Get in the driver's seat."

"Me?"

"Yes, you."

"I never did this before."

"Today's your day."

The tractor seemed so big. I slid off the fender and onto the driver's seat.

"I can't reach the brake pedal."

"Yes, you can. Just slide to the front of the seat."

"Okay, that's better."

"I can push the brake pedal."

I was DRIVING—in reality, I steered the tractor. Dad showed me how to use the hand clutch to stop power, and I could push the foot brake with my right foot to stop.

"Go ahead."

"Stop."

"You're going too far down the hill; turn the wheel to the right."

I thought I was cool. Talk about bragging rights. I had them when I went to first grade.

When a kid grows up on a farm, driving is like second nature. Eventually I worked into cultivating corn, raking hay and hauling manure. At age 14 I was allowed to drive the red Chevrolet pick-up truck and the dark blue 1952 Chevrolet sedan around the farm. All vehicles had a standard transmission.

One time, when I was 15, I tried to back the car out of the garage. I was going to drive the quarter-mile down the lane to get the mail and then drive back and put the car in the garage. Oops! You had to turn the steering wheel after backing out of the garage to head down the driveway. I turned the wheel too soon and caught the passenger side fender on the edge of the garage door frame. I couldn't get the car back into the garage without doing more damage, so I left it where it was. There was no doubt about who did this and there were no words to Dad that could help. Was my Dad angry? He was LIVID. The dent didn't affect how the car operated, but it was a constant reminder of the mishap because it was never repaired

My first on-the-road experience after I got my permit was to drive home from church with the entire family in the car—Dad, Mom, Curt and Gram. Talk about a car load of back-seat drivers! And none of them had a back-seat driver's license. I had trouble keeping the car on the road. It wanted to ride on the berm. Since I had never driven on the road, I had never had to keep within some given boundaries.

"Damn it—I'm not telling you to keep this car on the road again." Dad said in a low even voice.

"I'm trying."

I said something about Dad using swear words after leaving church. When would I learn not to upset the driving instructor?

Before it was time to take the test, I learned how to keep the car within the margins of the road.

My brother Curt, who is two years older than I am, had been a perfect student driver. He is still an excellent driver. I was happy when my dad didn't compare me to him, but in the back of my head, I compared myself to him.

Mom never had a driver's license and neither did Gram, so dad was the only person who took me for practice driving. I hadn't had my permit very long when Dad took me to Canonsburg. It was the first time I drove in town. After crossing the railroad tracks on Central Avenue, the road takes a slight grade.

"There's a parking place. Park there."

I didn't want to manipulate the car into the space; I hadn't parallel parked in town although I had set up a practice space at the farm. Of course, that's easy. There are no cars to interfere with the lines drawn on the driveway. I passed the parking space and came to the traffic light.

"Now go around the block and come back and park there."

"Maybe that space will be gone when I get around the block."

"Yikes! It's still empty."

I remembered the process for parallel parking and jockeyed the car into the space. My Dad got out and looked. He said. "That's really a half-assed job of parking."

I was just glad to have gotten the car into the space.

My driving improved all the time and I went to take my test on the first Monday morning after school was out in 1959. I drove with my dad to the Driver's Exam Center, located behind the Pennsylvania State Police Barracks in Washington, Pennsylvania.

In 1959, you didn't have to have a physical exam, an eye test or be quizzed on the laws of the highway before you got your permit. When you arrived at the site for the driving test, the examiner asked you questions about the traffic laws and you looked into a machine to take the eye test. I had sent for my permit on my sixteenth birthday. It came in the mail along with a booklet of questions from the Department of Motor Vehicles. The examiner could ask any of 100 questions. I had studied the questions and asked my friends about them. I passed that test easily, but had trouble passing the eye exam. I do not have binocular vision, and when I looked in the eye machine, the picture of the sign was on the left side and the words on the right side. I told the examiner that there were no words on the sign. Since then I have learned that I can alternate eyes to make the sign have words.

I traveled around the course and followed the examiner's direction. As we pulled toward the end of the path, he told me to ignore the stop sign because we could see that no one was coming. I didn't ignore the sign because my friends had told me this was a trick that the examiners often pulled on student drivers; it was a reason to fail the test.

The examiner asked me to stop on a short hill that led to where Dad was waiting. This was going to be difficult since I didn't like to start the standard shift on a hill. I bunny-hopped the car as I started.

"I just failed this test."

I continued up the hill and pulled to the spot where the examiner directed.

"What's dad going to say when he finds out I failed."

"Come with me." The examiner motioned.

We went to the spot where I had taken the eye test.

He stamped the permit twice and handed it to me; I was afraid to look.

When I peeked, I saw, "Passed" with the date written on the bottom. He also stamped—"Must Wear Corrective Lenses" below it.

"Yeah, I did it."

I was still taking piano lessons at that time and was to be at my teacher's house at 1:30 p.m. Gram thought that even though I had passed my test that morning she should go with me. As luck would have it, her cousin from Nebraska dropped in to visit and she couldn't go with me. This time I parked on the level on Central Avenue in Canonsburg. I was a solo driver.

43. MY FIRST BUSINESS

I was going to become an entrepreneur. I didn't even know what the word meant. But, I was going into the grass cutting business. The only problem was that I didn't have a lawn mower. I didn't have any customers and I didn't have a way to get from my house to possible clients. This was before the days of lawn cutting services, so grass cutting jobs were available. After all, the only money I had ever earned was what Curt and I got from selling strawberries. I didn't get paid for jobs I did at home, but my Mom and Dad did give me money when I asked, like when I went to the county fair or a high school football game.

A friend of mine had a small business of cutting yards in Canonsburg. He had a rotary mower that he pulled around backward as he rode his bicycle. He held the mower handle with one hand and guided the bike with his other hand. When he arrived at his client's house, he was set to cut grass. Living six miles from the nearest town prevented a town lawn cutting business.

My first yard-related job was cutting grass, raking leaves and trimming around the tomb stones at the Hill Church Cemetery. I earned one dollar per hour. This was one of the most boring things I ever did. The only benefit was the amount of information that I collected as I walked amongst the grave stones. Sometimes I had to crawl when I used hand clipper to cut around the tombstones. *I think I'll invent a Weed Wacker.* At one time, I could remember the birth and death dates of many deceased friends and relatives. The guy who was in charge of the cemetery always lurked around as though he was trying to find me loafing.

One of the things I did to combat the boredom was to listen to my transistor radio, which I carried in an inside pocket with an ear piece. He told me I shouldn't be listening because he thought it distracted me from doing the job well.

Although I didn't work there long, I was like a supervisor. I had a lot of people under me. Duh!

The second job was cutting grass and doing odd jobs for my Dad's cousin Margaret. I also helped her with digging and planting flowers and vegetables.

Cousin Margaret lived about ten miles from our house, but I was 16 and allowed to drive to her house. The first day I worked the whole day and instead of paying me, she gave me an old radio that I had admired. I was not real happy about this situation, but I didn't complain. Remember, I was working for a relative, and we really hadn't agreed on how much money she would pay me. The lesson: be careful what you admire. It was money that I was expecting, not an old used radio.

Margaret had what is known as a reel type lawn mower which is similar to a push mower that was used before power mowers. Her yard had a lot of plantain, a weed with a with a seed pod at the end of a very strong stem. Margaret's reel mower pushed the woody, stemmed plants to the ground when it passed over them, but it would not cut them off; the stems just popped back up. Fortunately, it did cut the grass around them.

When the job was done, Margaret remarked about how bad the yard looked with the leftovers that dotted the lawn. She knew that my family had a rotary mower, the one with a rotating blade that parallels the ground and runs at a much faster RPM.

"Do you think you could bring your mower with you the next time you come? That way you can cut the plantain weeds."

"I'll ask my dad."

My dad told me in no uncertain terms that I was not to take the lawn mower.

I took it anyway.

Dad's not home. He'll never know I used the mower. I'll be home before he gets back.

I took the mower fit nicely in the trunk, with the handle sticking out. A short piece of rope held the trunk lid down as I sailed down Route 19. I was in business.

Everything went well. I had nearly finished. Then it happened. I hit a small stump that had been sawed off very close to the ground, but not close enough to miss the mower blade.

CLUNK!

I'd hit a stick before. It's just the noise it makes.

As I proceeded, the plantains were still standing.

Then I looked back; nothing was getting cut.

I turned the mower off and tipped it onto its back wheels so that I could look under the mower.

OH NO! The blade was lodged against the mower frame. The stump had broken the shaft that connected to the mower engine. The blade was dragging along under the frame.

My dad's going to kill me. How will I ever tell him?

Margaret came from the back porch where she was sipping iced tea to see what was going on. She asked me if I wanted some tea.

My mouth was dry, not because I was thirsty, but because I was scared.

I told her what had happened, but she didn't seem interested. It was my problem.

"I think I better go home."

She paid me two dollars for the mowing I'd done.

What am I going to tell my Dad? He'll kill me.

Dad wasn't home when I got there, so there was more time to fret. I hadn't told my mom what happened. She hadn't known that I took the mower.

When would be the best time to tell him, probably at supper while everybody could hear the news? It might be easier than one to one. He wouldn't be as hard on me.

I was hungry, but I couldn't eat. Then just in time for peach cobbler, I got enough nerve.

"Dad, I took the mower to Margaret's so I could cut the plantain."

He said nothing.

"The shaft broke off when I hit a stump."

He didn't say a word, but I could read his face. Dad was not happy. But that wasn't the worst of it. He didn't say anything. Not a word, ever. I would have felt better if he had chewed me out a little bit. After all, I had disobeyed. I heard him talking to my mother about this when I came into the living room later in the evening. They stopped talking when I came in.

Dad got the new parts, tore the mower apart and repaired the broken shaft. All of this was done where I could see the unnecessary work I had caused him—let alone the money for parts. This punishment was worse than paying for the parts or getting a tongue-lashing about not listening.

Dad often rehearsed what he was going to say to somebody about something that bothered him, but he seldom knew how to have a real conversation. I think I heard him having one of these conversations with me while he repaired the mower.

My lawn mowing business was over.

44. I GOT TO DRIVE TO SCHOOL

My Dad always did the morning farm work, but for some reason, he was away and I had to do the milking on a fine fall morning. The year was 1960. One problem - I didn't get done in time to shower and catch the "on time" school bus. *What was I to do?*

My mother, who didn't drive, told me that I could drive the old 50s Dodge, Fluid Drive pick-up truck to school. WOW! I had hit it big. I had never been allowed to drive to school. It was the "day of days." *I'm driving to school.*

Although I was late to school, it was not a problem with the central office. I had to report to tell them that I was tardy and to register my truck. No biggie. *Wait till my lunch table gang hears this.* I drove to school

Even though Mr. English teacher got uptight and gave kids a hard time about coming late, it didn't bother me. I drove to school.

The Dodge truck was not the "truck limo" of today's truck line. I have friends and relatives who now have fancy trucks that are carpeted, with Bluetooth phone, stereo systems that make country music sound like it was produced in Carnegie Hall and seats that have 55 adjustments. These trucks have never had to haul cargo and NEVER will.

My dad bought this dirty green truck from the friend of a friend who told him how great a "buy" it was. A Great Buy? If it was such a great buy, then why did it need a new head light, new assembly for the parking lights, a small side window, new grill parts and an emergency brake because it didn't work—especially in emergencies? The new light assembly was attached to the truck in its primed color of drab gray. No dirty green paint for this new part. This was a work truck. It became known as a beater truck. A limo it was not. I drove a work truck to school.

No carpet in this truck. No radio in this truck. I was just glad that the hand crank for each window worked properly and the "wing" window didn't leak on rainy days. This truck hauled sacks of feed, parts for tractor repair, lumber, and it provided a country ride. It worked very well as the farm beater truck, but I drove it to school. It was licensed to drive on the road. Some farm trucks are for farm use only.

Don, at my lunch table, wasn't impressed when the lunch time talk got to my driving to school. After all, he drove to school every day so that he could go directly to the family's pet store where he cleaned cages. My driving to school didn't seem to impress anybody at the table, but I drove to school.

Then I saw Mary. We had been in school together since third grade.

"Hey Mary," I yelled to her where she sat at a girls' table near my guys' table. "Do you want to ride home with me?"

"You drove to school?"

"Meet me by the flag pole in front of the school. My truck's in the second row."

Mary and I had gone to the Sadie Hawkins dance, studied together and been good friends for a long time. She had ridden with me in our blue '52 Chevy to the library and to some other outings with high school friends.

The afternoon classes in Algebra and Latin seemed to fly by. I was going to drive home with Mary.

We met at the flag pole and headed toward the truck. As we approached the truck, I realized the wrinkle in my plan.

"Where's your car?" she inquired.

"My Dad has it."

"What are you driving?"

"I have the Dodge truck."

"I think I'll ride the bus," She told me.

"The buses have already left," I told her.

"Why didn't you tell me that you were driving this junk?"

"I didn't think it mattered."

"I guess I'll have to ride in it."

Mary was not happy with my country ride.

She got in and all but held her nose. The truck did have an odor because it was a dairy farm truck.

"What's this?" she queried.

"That's my Dad's tool bag."

It was my grandmother's many pocketed old purse that was filled with a mix of odd tools that might be used to fix a broken truck.

"Why does he have it in here?"

"It's for emergencies."

I started the truck, released the emergency brake and moved the truck forward about a foot. I pulled the emergency again, and got out.

"Where are you going?" she asked.

"I have to remove the block from behind the front wheel."

"Why do you do that?"

"The emergency brake doesn't hold real well. The block of wood is a backup."

With the backup emergency brake removed, I got back into the truck and we were off. Mary was glad when she found an outdated *Washington Observer* on the floor, under the dirty work gloves. She picked it up and sat huddled behind it until we were off the school property.

She jumped out quickly when I stopped in front of her house.

When I asked her to go to the prom, she asked, "What are you driving?"

45. HELP, THE SKY IS FALLING

"What's that noise? Is there someone in here?"

"It came from the dining room," Mom said. "Go see what it is."

"Help," I yelled to my mom as I walked from the kitchen to the dining room.

"What's wrong?" she asked.

"The new ceiling tiles are falling off the ceiling!"

"What did you do?" she asked.

"I didn't do anything," as I searched for something like a broom handle to hold back the tide of falling tiles.

There was no solution. It was an impossibility. We didn't have enough props. The tiles kept falling, first one at a time and then whole sections.

Neighbor Alvin Baker had spent a late winter Saturday installing a state-of-the-art tiled ceiling in the family dining room. The tiles locked together, but they still needed to be glued to hold them in place. This was the wonderful fiberglass tile that would cover the old flaking, painted ceiling that the oldsters in my family hated. I never noticed it. I guess I didn't look up. Mr. B. started early in the morning thinking that he could get the job completed before five o'clock. He had gone home and now Mom and I had to deal with the falling tiles. Dad and Curt were at the barn, taking care of the evening chores.

"Go get your dad," Mom ordered me.

"What's he going to do," I asked.

"Go get him."

Dad came in and surveyed the new ceiling.

"Stack the fallen ones in the corner, but don't let the glue sides touch each other," He urged. He didn't get excited.

And stack we did. They stood up at angles like the capital letter A, waiting for the Domino Effect to take over. It never did, but we tiptoed around our dining room over the weekend.

On Monday, Dad went to the Eighty Four Lumber outlet in Eighty Four, Pennsylvania, which was then a five-year-old company. He took the numbers from the tile boxes, took the cans that contained the glue and talked with the manager of the store. They were not prepared to deal with the problem, but wrote down all the information. The representative from their supplier would be in touch with dad to see what could be done about the falling tiles.

We eventually scraped the drying glue from the fiberglass pieces and stacked them in the outdoor shed. Some were broken, but most remained in one piece. Two companies were involved—one for tile and one for the glue. The tile company could find no problem with the tile. It took the glue company a little longer, but they came through. It was discovered that somewhere in transit the glue had been stored in a railroad boxcar where it had frozen. By freezing, it had lost its stick-to-it-ive-ness.

The Eighty Four Lumber Company was most helpful in dealing with the problem. All the tiles were replaced as well as the glue—plus Mr. Baker's labor fees. When the new tiles were placed on the ceiling, Mr. B. used small nails. The tile have been overseeing the meals and family life of that dining room for over fifty years.

By the way, Mr. B. nailed the fallen tile to the rental house ceiling located on our family farm. In those days we didn't waste anything. We didn't know it was called recycling.

46. SCARY, SCARY NIGHT

I don't know whether it was because it was October or if it was because I was truly scared. People at school had been talking about Halloween and some of the activities that they had experienced at haunted houses and telling scary stories. I had thought I knew what a ghost was when I was a young kid. I had dealt with all that — ghosts don't exist.

Friends invited me to a Halloween party. I dressed as a fireman and went to their party. They told a story of a witch burning in a bed and had fake smoke wafting from the background. It seemed very real.

As I walked through their dimly lit house, I saw a guy sitting in a wheel chair with what appeared to be one leg. The man was wailing, "They've cut my leg off." He really was sitting on the leg that appeared to be amputated. Then when I went around the corner, a leg was bouncing up and down in the opening of the table like a lever pushing back and forth. It was really a guy lying on a cot with his leg pumping up and down between two card tables. Tablecloths made it appear as a leg bouncing in the opening, while looking for its body.

And finally, we had to put our hands in a container that had large grapes floating freely in vegetable oil. We were told that in the next room, some guy was gouging people's eyes out. Oh, the power of suggestion. These ideas were all fresh in my mind since the party had been the previous weekend.

I had been to my Aunt Sally's house for the evening. She had given me a paper shopping bag full of yarn, small pieces of material and embroidery floss. The materials were for my mother who would use the cloth for a crazy quilt and would use the odds and ends of yarn to crochet afghan squares.

I had my own car, a black and white '57 Chevy Bel Air, but I had to park in the garage that was the farthest from our house. My dad and my brother had the preferred parking. After all I was the last to get a car and I was just glad to have a garage at all. It's very nice to have a garage when the weather is frosty or it is snowing.

As I got out of the car, I upset the gift bag that my Aunt had given me. After getting all the contents back in the bag, I headed toward the house. The dim outside light didn't provide much assistance to see the walkway into the house. I had walked this a thousand times. I could even do it in the dark. I often did. On this night I felt that someone was following me. I stopped and turned as quickly as I could to see who was behind me. (I wondered if someone was watching. I didn't want to appear afraid.) I saw no one. Had someone been lurking in the garage? What did they want from me? I didn't hear anybody. I didn't see anybody. Visions of Ichabod Crane passed through my head as I pictured "Sleepy Hollow" in my secluded lane just off Wilson Road. After all, we referred to the creek that ran behind the barn just below the railroad as the back hollow. The previous weekend's party activities still lurked in my head.

My mind was playing tricks on me. I tried to take another step. This time I couldn't move. I gave another quick turn of my head. Who's behind me? I stopped again. I yelled out, "Who are you?" There was no answer. I stopped in my tracks and tried to back up. I couldn't. I felt pretty silly yelling to the night. Then there's always the idea that my brother is waiting around the other garage and playing some kind of trick on me. I continued to search for the attacker or the reason that I couldn't move my feet.

If I can't walk ahead, maybe I can go back to the car. *I know, I'll start over.*

I tried to walk back to the car, but I couldn't move. Now I was really frightened. I couldn't move my feet. While keeping my eye on the house, I tried to turn again. I couldn't. I bent over to the ground and put my hands there to try to balance myself. I felt as if I was going to fall down but I did keep from falling, for the moment. As I tried to straighten up, I lost my equilibrium and fell to my knees and eventually was seated on my sit bones. It was then that I realized that my ankles were stuck together. Why couldn't I get them apart?

Now I'm sitting on the ground and running my hand down my ankles as I lean on the other hand so that I won't topple over. How did I get here? What is going on? I still can't move my legs. It's too dark. I can't see anything that is keeping me in this position. *Should I yell for my mom or dad? They'd never hear me. The TV is too loud to hear any outside noise.*

I kept on feeling around on the gravel surface for something—anything—I could identify. Finally I felt something that seemed like a piece of baler twine. Although there was a lot of baler twine around, there shouldn't be any here on the ground.

How silly of me. I traced the cord-like substance and at last realized that I was holding a strand of rug yarn in my fingers. How did this get here? Ah-hah! Now it all makes sense. I didn't pick up all the yarn from Aunt Sally, and it seemed that I had become entangled. I hadn't gotten everything in the bag when it upset. I wasn't "hog tied" after all. The ghosts weren't flying and there were no black cats trying to cross my path. There's no Halloween cat after my soul or no ghost on Wilson Road. WHEW!

47. HIND SIGHT

It was the summer of 1963. I wanted my own car. My cousin Jim Myers and I scoured the free newspaper for the perfect one.

"Look at this Keith. It's a '57 Chevy and it's in Mt. Lebanon."

"I bet it's a convertible like Dinah Shore rode in when she sang, "See the USA in Your Chevrolet. . . "

"Wow! Wouldn't that be cool?"

So, I called and we could see it the next day. As we neared the house, there sat the car. It was every teenager's dream. It wasn't a convertible. But it was shiny black. It had racing slicks. It had a raised hood. It had dual exhausts. It even had fuzzy dice hanging from the rear view mirror. This car oozed testosterone.

"My Dad'd kill me if I brought this car home," I said to Jim.

"We're here. We have to check this out," Jim said.

And we did. Jim loved the car. When he lifted the hood and saw the engine, he was hooked.

Jim eventually bought that car. This high-powered, decked-out racer shook the ground when it started, and the wheels chirped on the pavement when the clutch was engaged. He spent a lot of money "souping it up," so he could drag race it legally. He had a lot of trophies and a thinner wallet to prove it.

As word got around that I was looking for a car, Burdette, the guy who trucked our milk, told my Dad that his wife was selling her car.

"Yeah, it's probably an old lady's pink Ford," I complained."

"I think Mr. Burdette said it's a '57 Chevy."

"It could still be an old lady car."

My dad called Mrs. B. and made arrangements to see the car that evening.

"Wow! Look at that car. I'll buy it." I said as we drove in and I saw the black and white sedan.

Even though it wasn't the highest end of the model, I could see myself driving it.

Dad said, "It could be a clunker."

I drove it. I loved it. I wanted it.

When we got out of the car after the test drive, I asked, "How much do you want for it."

"$700." She quickly answered.

I looked at Dad and he nodded his head. *I'm getting my own car.*

This time, I went to Mellon Bank, as opposed to "The Bank of Dad." I withdrew my graduation money, my money from cutting the cemetery grass and my money from Christmas gifts. This left $5 in my savings account.

Mrs. B., Dad and I went to our insurance office where the secretary filed papers for the transfer of the title.

When the secretary asked about insurance, Dad said, "Add his car to my policy, that way he won't have to pay any additional insurance."

One of the benefits of living on a farm is "Dad's Gas and Oil Company," which is supposed to supply tractors and other farm vehicles. We all used it.

In 1966, I traded the '57 Chevy for a new 1966 V.W. Bug.

How did I know that this "little old lady car" would become a collector's car and be worth as much as $60,000 today?

What is it about hindsight and vision?

My parents, Frank James Neill and Mary Eliza Myers Neill
   early 1940s

The picture below was taken on the side porch of the Eighty Four farm house during the summer of 1950.

1. my brother Curtis (Curt) Neill, 2. my grandmother, Jane Mary Washabaugh Neill, 3. me, Keith Neill, 4. Cousin Jim Myers, 5. my aunt Sarah Neill Myers, also known as Aunt Sally, 6. cousin Jane Myers, later last name Moon, 7. my father Frank Neill, 8. My mother Mary Myers Neill.

Below Sisters Great Aunt Grace Washabaugh Carson, my Grandmother Jane Mary Washabaugh Neill, Sarah Washabaugh Donley. Quilters 1950s.

My dad, Frank Neill picking corn Circa 1974

Sisters, Great Aunt Ella Sumney Williams and my Grandmother, Emma Jane Sumney Myers

My father Frank Neill, my mother Mary Eliza Myers Neill,
my brother Curtis (Curt) Neill and me, Keith Neill
Circa 1953